Rhetorics of Self-Making

Rhetorics of Self-Making

EDITED BY
Debbora Battaglia

UNIVERSITY OF CALIFORNIA PRESS
Berkeley   Los Angeles   London

University of California Press
Berkeley and Los Angeles, California

University of California Press
London, England

Copyright © 1995 by The Regents of the University of California

Library of Congress Cataloging-in-Publication Data

Rhetorics of self-making / edited by Debbora Battaglia.
    p. cm.
    Includes bibliographical references and index.
    ISBN 0-520-08798-4 (alk. paper).—ISBN 0-520-08799-2 (pbk. :
alk. paper)
    1. Self—Social aspects.   2. Self—Cross-cultural studies.
3. Ethnopsychology. I. Battaglia, Debbora.
BF697.5.S65R48 1995
155.2—dc20   94-398
                                            CIP

Printed in the United States of America
1 2 3 4 5 6 7 8 9
The paper used in this publication meets the minimum requirements of American
National Standard for Information Sciences—Permanence of Paper for Printed Library
Materials, ANSI Z39.48-1984 ∞

CONTENTS

ACKNOWLEDGMENTS / *vii*

1. Problematizing the Self: A Thematic Introduction
Debbora Battaglia / *1*

2. Self-Exposure as Theory: The Double Mark of the Male Jew
Jonathan Boyarin and Daniel Boyarin / *16*

3. On Eccentricity
George E. Marcus / *43*

4. If You Have the Advertisement You Don't Need the Product
Roy Wagner / *59*

5. On Practical Nostalgia: Self-Prospecting among Urban Trobrianders
Debbora Battaglia / *77*

6. Nostalgia and the New Genetics
Marilyn Strathern / *97*

7. Production Values: Indigenous Media and the Rhetoric of
Self-Determination
Faye Ginsburg / *121*

CONTRIBUTORS / *139*

INDEX / *143*

v

ACKNOWLEDGMENTS

The grant of an academic leave from Mount Holyoke College made it possible for me to undertake this project, and the generosity of the John Simon Guggenheim Memorial Foundation made it possible for me to complete it. I am grateful to George Collier and the Department of Anthropology at Stanford University for providing me with an institutional home during the gestation of the book. Warmest thanks to the authors of the chapters for their professional conduct and good will. And, as I have learned it is never needless to say, I am grateful to Bruce Bongar for his support on the domestic scene and to Brandon Bongar for keeping me in touch with what matters.

ONE

Problematizing the Self: A Thematic Introduction

Debbora Battaglia

There is no self alone at the start.
—PAUL RICOEUR

INVITING AMBIGUITY

This project began as an invitation to contributors to write on "the rhetoric of self-making" for annual meetings of the American Anthropological Association.[1] The topic was, of course, ambiguous (which I think it fair to say was an issue for us all) owing entirely to the place and effect of "rhetoric" in the title—its unsettling influence on "self" and "making." For taken here as ideology's "signifying aspect" (Barthes 1977, 49), rhetoric alerts us that the "self" cannot appear within these pages as a natural object, unproblematically given, or as an essential, preexisting sense to be fashioned (Greenblatt's starting point in his seminal study of Renaissance self-fashioning [1980]). Likewise, "making" cannot straightforwardly be taken as determining a self (an experience or realization of self may bear little relation to a self "made"), or as invariably useful for understanding how selfhood emerges in cultural practice. Thus, under rhetoric's influence, the self cannot be the stable product of its own manufacture (e.g., as in the "self-made man"). Indeed, the production of some *thing*, or even a multiplicity or a sequence of unitary self-objects or coherent self-images (since this position implies a self there or invariably worked toward at the beginning) is likely to appear beside the point of how to represent the nonsteady state of selfhood in different cultural situations, and varying degrees and relations of determinancy. And the plot thickens. For the authors, all of us anthropologists, are seeking to privilege subjects' modes of knowledge and experience—our roots in ethnography insist upon this—meanwhile acknowledging that our efforts have our own rhetorical traditions as their wellsprings, and comprise only one dimension of the discriminating enterprise of anthropology.[2]

1

"SELF" AS A REPRESENTATIONAL ECONOMY

A multiplicity of rhetorics shares, then, a place with a diversity of socialities as the only givens at the scene of writing. Hence our collective focus on rhetorical practices in contradistinction to finished products of rhetorical activity.[3] If this volume contributes furthermore to what might be termed a *critical anthropology of selfhood,* an anthropology emergent, that is, in the off-centering effects of a (structurally) ironic self-distancing, it is because its proper subject is neither the self (as experienced) nor the "self" (as culturally figured) but the *problematics of self-action* in their relation to issues of power. One might say that a focus on rhetoric does not allow one to *deny* problematic relationships their profile in argumentation; does not allow us to *oppose* destabilizing the cultural constructs it investigates. Accordingly, whether readers prepare to "suspend disbelief" or to be suspicious (as in Ricoeur's two strategies of rhetorical reading [1992, 159 n. 23]), the rhetorical awareness prefigured in the title does not allow a passive reading of the ambiguities or the cultural mediations at hand.[4]

Too, this volume turns away from issues of textual eloquence; it is not about the "commanding dominance of the individual personality" in some consummate performance or text (Kant's observation in *Kritik der Urteilskraft,* reiterated by Nietzsche [1983, 97]). Instead, rhetoric is taken as an uncertain and provisional social project. Insofar as this project is characterized by a blurring of "the limit separating expression from disguise, but also [allowing] that oscillation succinct expression" (Barthes 1977, 57), its aesthetic has less to tell us about style in some pure form than about the political judgments it inscribes.

From this position there is no selfhood apart from the collaborative practice of its figuration. *The "self" is a representational economy:* a reification continually defeated by mutable entanglements with other subjects' histories, experiences, self-representations; with their texts, conduct, gestures, objectifications; with their "argument of images" (from Fernandez, as discussed by Ewing [1990, 265]), and so forth. Marilyn Strathern has described the "integratory capacity" (1991, 15) of such summary concepts—their effect (as with ethnography) of producing an experience or evoking an image of integration which nonetheless fails to encompass the diversity of possible experiences. Selfhood by this figuration is a chronically unstable productivity brought situationally—not invariably—to some form of imaginary order, to some purpose, as realized in the course of culturally patterned interactions.

From this perspective the "transcendent self" of ego psychology and some psychological anthropology, a self perduring, continuous, impermeable, unitary, and universally sought after (for discussion, see Murray 1993, 3), is cast as a socially enacted agenda or ideology, a practical capacity of human culture rather than of human nature. We are left, then, to challenge any a priori valuation of transcendence on methodological grounds at least. Further, we come to appreciate the close relatedness of a unitary self-concept and rhetorics of individuality. For the ethnography makes it apparent that alternative constructs exist—different premises of self-experience—as practices that inscribe *dividuality* (Strathern's important insight [1988]) as a culturally valued capacity of persons. This is most apparent where the ethnographic focus shifts to exchanges of objects that, whether as gifts or as commodities, are seen to engender and concretize subjects' attributes (Battaglia, this volume)[5] over the course of their social life. The cultural mechanisms of displacement, deferral, extension, projection or introjection, and so forth, by which this process operates, call to issue any ascription of inherent value to such objects, and analogously, any assertion that self-centeredness or a singular "self identity" is universally desirable. Instead, subjects may concern themselves with the social possibilities of attaching and detaching material self-objectifications; of maintaining a multiplicity of sources of self-influence in these concrete terms.[6] The placedness of the subject is important in this context, as are the dispersed habitation of the self in various forms and the effect this has of ramifying or prescribing sites of self-encounter. From this critical recognition, possibilities present themselves for cross-cultural comparisons of the structuration and subversion of selfhood rather than of "selves."

An approach to selfhood as an embodied and historically situated practical knowledge, in other words, prompts a larger question of rhetoric, namely, what *use* a particular notion of self has for someone or for some collectivity. It is this question that separates the working premises of authors here from a narrowly textual, Aristotelian regard for rhetoric "as one finds it in books," to cite Nietzsche's critique, "just as [Aristotle] also thinks the effect of drama to be independent of the performance, and thus does not take up the physical presence on stage in its definition" (Nietzsche 1983, 100). And it gives this volume a positive relation to studies, such as certain studies of self-narrative, which stress the role of agency, and the social conditions of textual production and reception as revealing of "the ambiguity of authorship" (Rosenwald and Ochberg 1992, ix; also, Crapanzano 1980, 1992; Young 1983). Accordingly we find ourselves, with no little trepidation, proceeding along a course explicitly alternative to essentialist exposition. This course prescribes that our concerns must have directly to do with the historical circumstances, the poetics, and the power relations that define a selfhood emergent in sociality—with the "substitutive reversals," the "referential aberrations," the "figural potentiality" (De Man 1979), the "deflections" (Burke 1969) constitutive (and not merely expressive) of the self-in-process, and the hidden agents and agencies rhetoric implicates.

Overall, the chapters of the book cohere around two sets of rhetorical tensions that subjects' "self-actions" (Wagner's term in this volume) present as critical issues: namely, locating agency, and rhetorics of individuality and relationality. At the same time, tensions exist within these issues which articulate telling cultural differences. I turn now to discussion of these.

LOCATING AGENCY: SELFHOOD AND DETERMINANCY

A salient theme of the studies that follow is the indeterminacy of rhetorical action. And it alerts us that the problematics of agency will be central to the process of signification that self-rhetoric manifests. In particular, we shall need to attend to the location of agency and the social conditions of its appearance or obfuscation. The critical point in this regard is that self-action may take place upon a subject apart from it; self-action may be oriented to or simply find its object and significance in a subject who is not its source. Put another way, the acting subject is not invariably or always consciously its own source of an experience or recognition of selfhood, or of a sense of herself or himself as fashioned. The story of the cultural mediation of this experience or sense is the story of rhetoric's originative force.

Here issues of technology enter in directly. If we accept that the problematic of agency is central to theorizing selfhood, then we must take account of what Foucault terms "technologies of self": that is, the instrumental means and practices of self-action as understood historically. Technologies of self, which "can be found in all cultures in different forms . . . , do not require the same material apparatus as the production of objects; therefore they are often invisible techniques" (1984, 369). This invisibility is an important factor when considering the ethics and effects of self-rhetoric in context of the conditions and issues of postmodernity. Where new technologies stand to place not only persons' disembodied images but their genes "on stand by" (Heidegger 1977, 17) for possible use by others, the Platonic aim that a life become a work of art is profoundly challenged. Foucault wrote (shortly before his death): "From the idea that the self is not given to us, I think that there is only one practical consequence: we have to create ourselves as a work of art" (1984, 350–351). Yet where the forces of biotechnologies and information technologies hold sway, that vision is qualified, as it were, where it lives. The ancient Greek "kind of ethics which was an aesthetics of existence" (Foucault 1984, 343)—and which was not special to the Western world—is called to relinquish the skin-bound individual as its primary site of moral control; to resituate or reinvest morality in relational flows that extend beyond such boundaries of the flesh.

George Marcus begins his chapter on this point by critiquing the notion of a self "made" other than rhetorically. Arguing for the eccentric self as a "thoroughly performative, sensorial, unself-conscious response to the social conditions that define one's selfhood—conditions that involve hidden . . . agency," he calls attention to the position of self-agents and agencies between the eccentric person's sense of self and that of the eccentric's public. As "taken over" by these mediating influences, the self is "mimetically doubled or parallel"—locatable as its doppelganger, a mere "familiar" abiding most certainly in this representation without structural equivalence to an original model. Indeed, eccentrics are "hyper-aware that their selves are being created elsewhere, in an unseen world." The imaginary, then, is the only stable component of this self-action (a point that calls to mind Nietzsche's philosophical position on rhetoric). An operation of the "radical displacement of self in sentience," it is brought to substitute for self-awareness by its public's indulgence of the mechanisms of image production.

Of course, audiences indulging others' self-images, or for that matter responding skeptically to them, are actively (though not necessarily knowingly) committing their own self-action. It becomes important in this regard to know if audience self-action is affected by the degree or location of control of the rhetoric. That is, do audiences respond differently to a doppelganger produced by external agencies than to images whose production is seized in self-awareness? The case of Aboriginal filmmakers illuminates some further implications of this question. For, as Faye Ginsburg shows, indigenous producers are acting upon their awareness of hidden agency in taking control of their own image production. Introducing their rhetoric and goals into an existing global industry, they become coproducers with governments responsible for the political circumstances against which the media asserts itself. It is this ironic and ambivalent coproduction embodied in the person of the filmmaker as a "bush cosmopolitan" which evokes for Euro-American audiences a vision of reconciliation which potentially masks inequality. They indulge not so much the agents' as their own imaginary identities.

When Roy Wagner states the point for advertising—that is, that advertising a "self" cannot be mistaken for performing a self—it is likewise to underscore the argument that self-awareness is not necessary to self-action. By his examples, self-enactments are realized in self-consumption, where agents reveal not their effectiveness as "hidden persuaders" so much as their capacity for persuading themselves of their effectiveness in shaping an identification in their audience. From this position, the self enacted is "nobody's vision." Being located, "unowned," in the advertising, the self has "the autonomy of a shaman's spirit powers" to generate its own effectiveness.

Something of this autonomous life is presented in the urban Trobriand case, where self-images in the national press and in the form of indigenous yam displays evolve a "conversational publicity" on the theme of cultural identity between parties whose connection may never be accomplished nor even explicitly sought. Rather, identity issues are incorporated into, or rejected from, the flow of social discourse, back and forth across categories of Trobriand or national identity. Thus a nostalgic coproductivity comes to substitute for a self as a product of activity; selfhood being, on the one hand, authored at times and with unknowable consequences—prospectively—by others, and on the other hand, deferred and displaced by the actions of other subjects in respect to the images fixed in yams or in print. One consequence of Trobrianders "disavowing dependency" (to take Judith Butler's phrase, discussed by Jonathan and Daniel Boyarin) on two self-fronts (i.e., as "traditional" and as "nationals") by enacting the rhetoric of each against the other is to leave their images open to further appropriation by agents who may operate them either in or against the self-interest of the persons imaged; turning self-images in support of or against themselves. Trobrianders assert an overarching connective value for this nondeterminative narrative process, quite apart from the positive or negative quality of the connection or any actual or envisioned outcome.

As Marilyn Strathern has shown in exploring the phenomenon for Melanesian culture, the agent, or acting subject, may thus be less a locus for relationships than a "pivot of relationships . . . one who from his or her own vantage point acts with another's in mind." In this view "the object or outcome is their relationship, the effect of their interaction" (1988, 272) to be transformed or replicated. However, the self-action of agents may only influence, but does not insure, control over the outcome. As her chapter here shows, it is the *terms* of the effort which problematize the relationship by means of rhetorical assertions that represent as biologically given the identities of subjects in fact connected as "relatives." It follows that the subject who seeks a "true" personal identity (for self or on behalf of another) by reference to biological makeup alone, commits an erasure or diminishment of self-agency. Paradoxically, to give definitional status to coproducers' genetic presentiments through time and to the locus of genes is to diminish an agency that from the start defined itself as a social relational capacity—not as a location at the site of a person.

It is on this point of deferrals and displacements of self-significance through time that we turn to the example of Jewish male identity, and to marks on the body of no more fixed or invariably active significance than genetic traces within it. Boyarin and Boyarin discuss, for example, how the Jewish father's decision to have his child circumcised may be seen as a deferral of his own selfhood to a time of experienced communality. If self-enactment can be deferred—if "there is no subject prior to imitation," but rather "as a bundle of operated bodily signs, intentions, and actions it is distributed across a temporal weave" nonsequentially—then a unilinear progressive conception of time is inadequate to discuss it. Connections, the authors point out, "are not merely 'with the past' along a line of time, but rather multidirectional," effected within "empathetically expanded time." There can be no "self-made man" within such a consciousness.

RHETORICS OF INDIVIDUALITY/RHETORICS OF RELATIONALITY

Another major theme of the collection is the tension between rhetorics of an individuated, autonomous self and rhetorics of a collective or relational self. As presented here, these rhetorics sometimes, but do not invariably, oppose each other as the grounds of social action (as well as that action itself). That is, some situations produce the action of tacking between the two as incompatible positions, others of tacking between them as complementary positions, still others of appropriating one rhetoric to the cause of the other. The fact that rhetorical self-action within and across cultural boundaries can present this kind of porosity or disloyalty to fixed ideological definitions— running stubbornly contrary to the notion of unchanging cores of personal identity—indicates the larger problem with the self/other binary for comprehending the sociality of selfhood. Even when conceived of, very valuably I believe, as a dialectical (in the sense of a dialogical) relationship (e.g., Bakhtin 1981; Bruner 1984; Crapanzano 1992) or, after George Mead, as a social premise for redefining the "self" as a "self-other" (Mead 1962), conditions are created for "othering" which tend to neglect or underrepresent power asymmetries, and for the rhetoric—the "self" concept—to be conflated with self-experience. To note this danger is to invite critical consideration of why we or our subjects take up one rhetorical position or another, of to what feared or hoped-for effect we engage the rhetorics we do. Put another way, we must ask what effect one rhetoric engages another in relation to which it defines itself.

The fact that all the chapters analyze either Euro-American phenomena or

cultural action in their relation to Western dominance gives this query a purpose in examining the characterization of selves as culturally fated either to
relationality (e.g., Dumont 1972) or to individuality (e.g., Kohut 1971), or
as fixed cultural categories across contexts of social action (e.g., Geertz
1984). Indeed, it emerges from this volume that the equation of an individuated "self" with the "Western world" and the relational "self" with the "non-
Western world" is strikingly problematic—a rhetorical tension, quite possibly, of most approaches to the cross-cultural study of selfhood and not a
cultural given for subjects.[7] For the same dichotomy exists within Western
contexts, in this volume appearing as distinct Jewish and Christian American
ideologies of self and self-action (by reference to their respective historical
valuations of group identity and individual salvation [Boyarin and Boyarin];
see also Taylor 1989); within the person of the eccentric whose individuality
is, paradoxically, denied by the fact of multiple agents and agencies' involvement in authoring her or his "self" (Marcus); as tensions within feminist
scholarship and practice to do with issues of presenting gender relations as
culturally specific or "derelationalizing" women vis-à-vis masculinist ideologies (Strathern). And the point appears analogously in the "self-determination" movements of fourth-world and third-world peoples (Ginsburg) and
in the culturally elaborated slippage of individuated/relational ideologies of
self embodied by certain Trobriand figures, whose self-characterizations as
"revolutionaries" derive from the pervasive individualism of a postcolonial
urban context they occupied and exploited (Battaglia). Thus, as Robert Foster (n.d.) has recently argued, we must likewise attend to the various sites of
production and consumption—state, commercial, local, and so forth—at
which the body becomes "the site of apparently autonomous agency (free
will, free choice)" in contradistinction to a prevailing valuation of collectivity
and relationality.

    While critically reframing self typologies, these essays participate also in
exposing the inner self/outer self dichotomy as culturally and historically
specific—a point that historically has been explored in reference to cultural
constructs of emotion (see, e.g., Lutz 1988, Myers 1979, 1986; Rosaldo
1984; A. Strathern 1977; M. Strathern 1979). Of course, the reframing and
reinscription of these binarisms begs a larger question even as it turns our
attention to the border crossings—the problematic self-action—which make
such alterities apparent as rhetorical constructions. For while accepting that
bipolar types of self are "wildly overdrawn" in the anthropological and psychological literature (Spiro 1993, 117), and mind/body dualisms likewise,
the alternative of a self-practice model asserts itself here without apology
against the "transcendent self" concept (Murray 1993), in the voices of au-

thors who are most self-consciously reflexive. It is then the relation of folk models (e.g., of a "whole self," a "private self") to self-practices, as well as to Western theories that themselves divide along relational-individual lines, which remains to be explored (Spiro 1993). Implicitly, this volume calls for such exploration.

Ginsburg speaks powerfully to this issue in her discussion of the process she observed of Aboriginal media producers being commodified and valued as individual "auteurs" in the marketing of Australia's cultural image at home and overseas. Rather than their efforts being taken as representing the interests of a broader polity, indigenous filmmakers are thus submitted, as cultural capital, to the dominant culture's valuation of the individuated self in self-expression. As their own goals of self-determination for the broader polity are obscured and depotentiated in consequence—as a self-determination explicitly evocative of nationhood "implicitly suggests the merging of individual with collective interests" and "privileges the individual as a political or artistic agent, implicitly detached or even in opposition to a broader polity"— the "conflation of rhetorics" renders the apparent empowerment of indigenous filmmakers a mask for "current inequalities and a history of political domination and cultural destruction."

Issues of self-determination and a similar threat of subversion are implicitly central also in Strathern's discussion of the rhetoric of individuality in genetic essentialism. Moving us to the site of the body and to personal identity, Strathern shows that to posit genetic knowledge as the source of uniqueness denies social context and relational identity its rhetorical efficacy, presenting "as given what is in fact a culturally mediated, relational identity." In this context, Euro-American genetic essentialism "cannot be disavowed, but it can be disowned as partisan"—exposed as medico-legal rhetoric. As genetic manipulation and the construction of "genetic families" is arguably self-determination at its most avowed, basic, and literal, the notion of "self-determination" itself emerges as figurative, demanding of interpretation and rigorous scrutiny as an ideological notion, as well as an empirical effect.

In both of these cases, relational selfhood gains in value and significance in opposition to a rhetoric of individuation. But whereas, as Ginsburg states, "indigenous media has been able to flourish because of the space opened up by the contradictory rhetorics of self-making that shape its production reception in both dominant and Aboriginal cultures," genetic essentialism is expanding into the space that relationality increasingly occupies only as a nostalgia for tradition. In neither case can the opposing rhetorics be neatly discussed in terms of indigenous selves and nonindigenous others, or without acknowledging the possibilities for anthropological engagement to make apparent, as opposed to obfuscating, indigenous processes of self-identity.

Wagner reminds us of issues of national cultural identity in his discussion of "the kinds of cultural problems that advertising brings to the fore"—the substitution of image for effectiveness in contemporary America. This discussion centers on the notion that images of products which embody the idea of America are more important as emblems of the America idea than as material things. The paradox is that advertising rhetoric is a force of purely imaginary collectivization that, in creating a "need for need," a "negative artifact," gives an ideology of individuality and particular consumption the object necessary to its existence. Self-action, then, being predicated on a "contagious image of consumption," may be performed without self-awareness. The case in point is given as a "contingent America," predicated on the "self-action" of consumers who may act aware, but are not necessarily aware, of advertisers' intentions, and by the self-action of advertisers who do not reflect needs or wants of consumers so much as they mime their own heritage of product invention within the cultural imaginary of advertising. The concept of construction, of America as a cultural construct, is not necessary or adequate to this phenomenon of mutual attraction of subjects to their own objectifications in wholly contingent self-action.

The point begs a question for the urban Trobriand case, wherein the presentation of certain Trobrianders as "traditional" in the national press is problematic in respect to both their national and their Trobriand cultural identities. In the postcolonial urban context, even the cultural given of inherited relationship is construed as open to redefinition. Specifically, Trobrianders of low matrilineal rank appropriate the license of a postcolonial rhetoric of individuality and independence to assert new versions of themselves which effectively upend power relations as structured in the Trobriand hierarchy. This self-argument or self-prospecting on two fronts, in respect to identities both more and less traditional than as given by cultural convention, presents a Janus-action of resistance to individualistic and relational ideologies alike. Further, as the press images take on a significance and life of their own, "otherness" emerges in its multidimensionality as circumstantially and nondeterminantly external or internal relative to the self-in-process. For urban Trobriand elite, the answer to the question of who one is defining oneself against is thus always, at some point and of course only partially, "oneself."

Offering, alongside Ginsburg, a valuable shift to a broader historical perspective, Marcus shows how the families of eccentrics appropriate the eccentric individual identity as a "dynastic marker of distinctive status." This appropriative action, presenting as a legitimate reception of inheritance, a given relationship, shows the rhetoric of individuation taken to its logical extreme.

But this rhetoric depends for its effect on audience complicity. The general public must indulge a "discourse of distinction" in order for it to operate.

Jewish Orthodoxy presents a striking contrast in this regard. When Boyarin and Boyarin draw attention to the head covers of Orthodox Jewish males as marks of distinction, it is to make the point that "external others" may also be Jews—that otherness may be nonoppositional to some self-object—but also to suggest the effect of inscribing a "more profound unity that transcends . . . superficial differences." The authors' contestation of what they refer to as the "moral and political effects of 'othering' " (in this context, an expression of the choice to be native) sets out "the negotiation of pulls" toward individual and collective selfhood in the ritual action of Jewish males by describing this dynamic as a "critical posing of freedom" that is "imperfectly effected" in Judaism.

For anthropologists, a project that challenges essentialist notions is perhaps uniquely risky. For we are enjoined, as I mentioned earlier, to act upon the limits and potential of acknowledged coauthorship with indigenous subjects. There is, in other words, an inherent reflexivity, an implication of rhetorics across the frames of our and others' engagement in rhetorical action, from which there is no recusing ourselves as writers of culture who are also engaged in a comparative enterprise (Clifford and Marcus 1986; M. Strathern 1991). And this fact exists alongside a deep regard for subjects' positions which, as I have noted, ethnography stands for within or without the field of cultural studies. Furthermore, we must recognize that people may argue and persuade not only with words but with sounds and gestures and objects and the images produced by new technologies—which this particular collection highlights by its choice of topics. These require that we acknowledge the operation of material constraints across forms of rhetorical action, and the culture-specific values such constraints encode.

Fundamentally, the patterns of self-action which appear in these pages reveal the capacity of rhetoric to generate social "entanglement" (Ricoeur 1992, 161) and disentanglement, and to incorporate or externalize others. The poetics and the politics of selfhood converge on this point. But the studies themselves will tell it better.

NOTES

1. These meetings were held in San Francisco in 1992. Not all chapter authors presented papers on this occasion, and Susan Harding, Jean Lave, and Paul Rabinow, whose participation I acknowledge with gratitude, did not go on to contribute chap-

ters. I am grateful also to Nicholas Thomas especially and to James Weiner for their comments on the introduction (at a possibly too-late stage of its development).

2. For a conversation on the debate about anthropological authority in these terms, see for example Sangren 1988 (and attendent comments) and M. Strathern 1991.

3. Myers and Brenneis (1984) make this distinction explicit for their anthology from the Pacific.

4. Douglas (1975, 7) makes the point anthropologically in reference to "implicit meanings."

5. A considerable Melanesian literature has evolved along these lines (e.g., see Battaglia 1990; Clay 1986; Mosko 1983; M. Strathern 1988; Wagner 1986; Young 1983).

6. For example, Weiner (n.d.) explores the implications of this awareness for conceptualizing subject-object relations across European (Lacanian) and Melanesian (M. Strathern's, Wagner's) analytic paradigms. From South Indian women, Trawick (1990, 193) employs Kristeva's "abject-object" paradigm in an intriguing analysis of selves "defined negatively, as not this or that . . . [such that] the self . . . is by its very inception [by giving a name to itself] not whole. It feels itself to be incomplete and fragmented."

7. I hesitate to merely list the important collections and monographs that define the problem in these terms, since their significance, particularly and collectively, far exceeds the dimensions of the problem itself. The anthropological publications mentioned in recent essays on the topic by Murray (1993) and Spiro (1993) include Dumont 1985; Kondo 1990; Lutz 1988; Lutz and Abu-Lughod 1990; Marsella, DeVos, and Hsu 1985; Shweder and Bourne 1984; White and Kirkpatrick 1985.

REFERENCES

Aristotle. 1941. *The Basic Works of Aristotle.* Edited by Richard McKeon. New York: Random House.

Bakhtin, M. M. 1981. *The Dialogic Imagination: Four Essays.* Edited by Michael Holquist. Translated by Caryl Emerson and Michael Holquist. Austin: University of Texas Press.

Barthes, Roland. 1977. *Image, Music, Text.* Translated by Stephen Heath. New York: Noonday Press.

Battaglia, Debbora. 1990. *On the Bones of the Serpent: Person, Memory, and Mortality in Sabarl Island Society.* Chicago: University of Chicago Press.

Bruner, Edward, ed. 1984. *Text, Play, and Story: The Construction and Reconstruction of Self and Society.* 1983 Proceedings of the American Ethnological Society. Washington, D. C.: American Ethnological Society.

Burke, Kenneth. 1969. *A Rhetoric of Motives.* Berkeley and Los Angeles: University of California Press.

Clay, Brenda Johnson. 1986. *Mandak Realities: Person and Power in Central New Ireland.* New Brunswick, N.J.: Rutgers University Press.

Clifford, James, and George Marcus, eds. 1986. *Writing Culture: The Poetics and Politics of Ethnography.* Berkeley, Los Angeles, London: University of California Press.

Crapanzano, Vincent. 1980. *Tuhami: A Portrait of a Moroccan*. Chicago: University of Chicago Press.
———. 1992. *Hermes' Dilemma and Hamlet's Desire: On the Epistemology of Interpretation*. Cambridge: Harvard University Press.
De Man, Paul. 1979. *Allegories of Reading: Figural Language in Rousseau, Nietzsche, Rilke, and Proust*. New Haven, Conn.: Yale University Press.
Douglas, Mary. 1975. *Implicit Meanings: Essays in Anthropology*. London: Routledge and Kegan Paul.
Dumont, Louis. 1972. *Homo Hierarchicus*. London: Paladin.
———. 1985. "A Modified View of Our Origins: The Christian Beginnings of Modern Individualism." In *The Category of the Person: Anthropology, Philosophy, History*, edited by M. Carrithers, S. Collins, and S. Lukes, 93–122. Cambridge: Cambridge University Press.
Ewing, Katherine P. 1990. "The Illusion of Wholeness: Culture, Self, and the Experience of Inconsistency." *Ethos* 18:251–278.
Foster, Robert. 1993. "Bodies, Commodities, and the Nation-State in Papua New Guinea." Paper presented at the Association for Social Anthropology in Oceania annual meeting, Honolulu.
Foucault, Michel. 1984. "On the Genealogy of Ethics: An Overview of Work in Progress." In *The Foucault Reader*, edited by Paul Rabinow, 340-372. New York: Pantheon Books.
Geertz, Clifford. 1984. " 'From the Native's Point of View': On the Nature of Anthropological Understanding." In *Culture Theory: Essays on Mind, Self, and Emotion*, edited by R. A. Shweder and R. A. LeVine, 123–136. Cambridge: Cambridge University Press.
Ginsburg, Faye. 1987. "Procreation Stories: Reproduction, Nurturance, and Procreation in Life Narratives of Abortion Activists." *American Ethnologist* 14:623–636.
Greenblatt, Stephen. 1980. *Renaissance Self-Fashioning: From More to Shakespeare*. Chicago: University of Chicago Press.
Heidegger, Martin. 1977. *The Question Concerning Technology*. Translated by William Lovitt. New York: Harper and Row.
Kohut, Heinz. 1971. *The Analysis of the Self*. New York: International Universities Press.
Kondo, Dorinne K. 1990. *Crafting Selves: Power, Gender, and Discourses of Identity in a Japanese Workplace*. Chicago: University of Chicago Press.
Lutz, Catherine. 1988. *Unnatural Emotions: Everyday Sentiments on a Micronesian Atoll and Their Challenge to Western Theory*. Chicago: University of Chicago Press.
Lutz, Catherine, and Lila Abu-Lughod, eds. 1990. *Language and the Politics of Emotion*. Cambridge: Cambridge University Press.
Marsella, Anthony, George DeVos, and Francis Hsu, eds. 1985. *Culture and Self: Asian and American Perspectives*. New York: Tavistock Publications.
Mead, George Herbert. 1962 [1934]. *Mind, Self, and Society from the Standpoint of a Social Behaviorist*. Edited by C. W. Morris. Chicago: University of Chicago Press.
Mosko, Mark. 1983. "Conception, De-conception, and Social Structure in Bush Mekeo Culture." *Mankind*, Special Issue: *Concepts of Conception: Procreation Ideologies in Papua New Guinea*, edited by Daniel Jorgensen, 14:24–32.

Murray, D. W. 1993. "What Is the Western Concept of the Self? On Forgetting David Hume." *Ethos* 23:3–23.

Myers, Fred. 1979. "Emotions and the Self: A Theory of Personhood and Political Order among Pintupi Aborigines." *Ethos* 7:343–370.

———. 1986. *Pintupi Country, Pintupi Self: Sentiment, Place, and Politics among Western Desert Aborigines.* Berkeley, Los Angeles, London: University of California Press.

Myers, Fred R., and Donald Lawrence Brenneis. 1984. "Introduction: Language and Politics in the Pacific." In *Dangerous Words: Language and Politics in the Pacific,* edited by Donald Lawrence Brenneis and Fred R. Myers, 1–29. New York: New York University Press.

Nietzsche, Friedrich. 1983. "Nietzsche's Lecture Notes on Rhetoric: A Translation." Translated by Carol Blair. *Philosophy and Rhetoric* 16:94–129.

Ricoeur, Paul. 1992. *Oneself as Another.* Translated by Kathleen Blamey. Chicago: University of Chicago Press.

Rosaldo, Michelle. 1984. "Toward an Anthropology of Self and Feeling." In *Culture Theory: Essays on Mind, Self, and Emotion,* edited by R. A. Shweder and Robert LeVine, 137–157. Cambridge: Cambridge University Press.

Rosenwald, George C., and Richard L. Ochberg, eds. 1992. *Storied Lives: The Cultural Politics of Self-Understanding.* New Haven, Conn.: Yale University Press.

Sangren, Steven. 1988. "Rhetoric and the Authority of Ethnography: 'Post Modernism' and the Social Reproduction of Texts." *Current Anthropology* 29:405–435.

Shweder, Richard, and Edmund Bourne. 1984. "Does the Concept of the Person Vary Cross-Culturally?" In *Culture Theory: Essays on Mind, Self, and Emotion,* edited by R. A. Shweder and R. A. Levine, 158–199. Cambridge: Cambridge University Press.

Spiro, Melford. 1993. "Is the Western Conception of the Self 'Peculiar' within the Context of World Cultures?" *Ethos* 21:107–153.

Strathern, Andrew. 1977. "Why Is Shame on the Skin?" In *The Anthropology of the Body,* edited by John Blacking, 99–110. London: Academic Press.

Strathern, Marilyn. 1979. "The Self in Self-Decoration." *Oceania* 49:241–257.

———. 1988. *The Gender of the Gift: Problems with Women and Problems with Society in Melanesia.* Berkeley, Los Angeles, London: University of California Press.

———. 1991. *Partial Connections.* ASAO Special Publication. Savage, Md.: Rowman and Littlefield.

Taussig, Michael. 1993. *Mimesis and Alterity: A Particular History of the Senses.* New York: Routledge.

Taylor, Charles. 1989. *Sources of the Self: The Making of the Modern Identity.* Cambridge: Harvard University Press.

Trawick, Margaret. 1990. "Untouchability and the Fear of Death." In *Language and the Politics of Emotion,* edited by Catherine Lutz and Lila Abu-Lughod, 186-206. Cambridge: Cambridge University Press.

Wagner, Roy. 1977. " 'Speaking for Others': Power and Identity as Factors in Daribi Mediumistic Hysteria." *Journal de la Société des Océanistes* 56–57:145–152.

———. 1986. *Asiwinarong: Ethos, Image and Social Power among the Usen Barok of New Ireland.* Princeton: Princeton University Press.

Weiner, James. n.d. "The Little Other Myth: For a Lacanian Approach to New Guinea Ritual." Manuscript. University of Manchester.

White, Geoffrey, and John Kirkpatrick, eds. 1985. *Person, Self, and Experience*. Berkeley, Los Angles, London: University of California Press.

Young, Michael. 1983. *Magicians of Manumanua: Living Myth in Kalauna*. Berkeley, Los Angeles, London: University of California Press.

TWO

Self-Exposure as Theory:
The Double Mark of the Male Jew

Jonathan Boyarin and Daniel Boyarin

*On the stand Chief Flying Eagle often sounds like a social studies teacher; his
speech is loaded with pat anecdotes and homilies.*

*Only once, toward the end of his testimony, does he do something unexpected.
Asked whether he often wears Indian regalia, Mills answers no, only at pow-
wows. Then he suddenly tugs at his necktie, pulling two thin strings of beads
from under his shirt. One, he says, is turquoise, from the Southwest. The other
small strand was a gift from his father.*

*Many people in the courtroom are surprised by this apparently spontaneous
revelation—surprised and, as Mills stuffs the beads back into his shirt and
fumbles to readjust his tie, a little embarrassed.*

—JAMES CLIFFORD

I

This is a semilegendary narrative told by two native brothers to each other.
Our purpose is to inquire into the formation of strong ethnic self-identification in a culture in which totality is already displaced or, put another way, to
ask how cultural relativists can have culture. Moreover, we wish to raise seriously the issue of how ethnic cultural identity can be constructed without the
pernicious moral and political effects of "othering." We will be using ourselves and each other as participant informants. The central metaphor for our
analysis is the "double sign" of Jewish male ethnic identity, one inscribed on
our genitals before we were ever able to exercise will, the other placed upon
our heads in a free-willed if ambivalent act of self-identification with ethnicity
which we carry with us into such social spaces as anthropology conventions.[1]
We will of course address the androcentric nature of both of these "signs"
and the troubling questions that it raises.

There are two parts to this chapter as well. The first tends to a focus on
circumcision and the historical context of early Judaism, hence to the "given"
in personal identity. The second, structured in response to a concise and
cogent statement about pluralism and "strong identity" by a leading political

theorist, draws largely on contemporary personal vignettes and has more to say about the head covering. Yet our choice of anecdotes and contexts within a broad sweep of Jewish textuality and experience is largely intended to subvert the common assumption that the given in identity is linked to domination, while the chosen necessarily implies free choice, noncoercive of others.

Perhaps an appropriate departure is the word "native," which we used in our first sentence. It could be objected that we are cloaking ourselves in the rhetoric of "authentic" knowledge of a bounded and *sui generis* culture. *Native* bears the traces of the imperial, territorializing context in which it became part of anthropology. Its history is that of the effort to create a unique mapping of human groups onto the globe, to separate and order them and keep them in their places (see, e.g., Fabian 1983; Ratzel 1898; J. Boyarin 1992). What would it mean to imply, as we do here, either that some of us are indeed natives (and some are not), or that one can choose consciously to be a native? In this case the answer has to do with a more specific return to the connections with birth implied by nativity. We understand ourselves as more profoundly born to, native to, an anamnestic generational tradition than to any national state or territory. The mark on our bodies, it seems to us, works harder than our birth certificates. Partly for that reason, we have chosen to affirm this mark in its detachable double, the head covering that identifies us as observant Jews.

If we stopped here, however, we would never get to the American Anthropological Association, which is hardly a forum for the shoring up of totalizing identities, whether "illusory" or "essential." Seeing ourselves as preplaced and placing ourselves within the tradition, we are also cognizant of the demands expressed by Walter Benjamin's dictum that "in every era the attempt must be made anew to wrest tradition away from a conformism that is about to overpower it" (Benjamin 1969, 255). This threatening conformity within Jewish discourse is to be found outside us—for example in the decidedly nontraditional Gush Emunim idolatry of the Land of Israel, which applies biblical rhetoric toward a thoroughly modernized version of territorialist nationalism (Lustick 1988; Schwartz 1992). More subtly we hope, but certainly more significantly for this discussion, the threat of conformity is also within us. There is a measure of imposition, a kind of symbolic violence or at least cognitive dissonance, induced by our exhibitionist or tricksterlike appearance as "Orthodox" Jews in such unorthodox settings. More systematically, the marks we ground our selfhood in are only imposed on and available to male Jews—although in nonorthodox communities women are increasingly adopting the yarmulke—and hence they are inescapably inscriptions of hierarchizing and reifying difference. There is also a danger that we will be tempted to push our stance in this chapter into the rhetorical presentation of a male duo who, through the powerful operations of some Kantian or Socratic self-critique, have managed to exorcise the difference between them.

The exigency of our times lays out the general agenda for our tradition of rescue work. We work at creating, "within" the tradition (for at some point we cannot escape spatializing metaphor), space for the autonomous existence of the sexual and ethnic Other. But it is inherent precisely in our public identification with a specific, rather than generically humanist tradition, that the creative outcomes of this rescue work are always contingent, rather than functionally predictable—hence the episodic and even decontextualized character of some of the ethnography herein. Nor do we necessarily suppose that we are pioneering what will become a new, hegemonic mode of Jewish self-imagining. While it has long been recognized that even in ancient times, "each generation had first to become Israel" (von Rad 1962, 162), it becomes somewhat difficult, given the increasing fragmentations of our times, to claim that in every time and place, Jews combine tradition and contemporaneity to produce a sum total that is "Israel." Although Jewish identification remains defined as an identification with other Jews, the fissures in such a corporate ideology are painfully obvious. Here, in fact, we focus more on corporeal than corporate identity.

Recognizing the artifice and power of the specific form of postmodern self-fashioning that leads us to emphasize Judaism in our own selves, we see our work as the opening of a nonreified difference in the space between the circumcision and the yarmulke-kipa-skullcap. We seek not to occupy a marginal position purified to a point, along the model of the solitary modern hero, but rather to travel along a marginal trajectory providing a connecting thread among an ever-widening field of articulated differences. In order for such a marginal trajectory to be traversable, it must be moored in the past, oriented toward a future however generally sensed, and given dimension by identifications with others in the present.[2] Put another way, in order for the margins to exist at all, they must have some content that affords them the possibility to resist pressure from the margins to evacuate or implode. Margins therefore produce their own centralizing and conformist pressures. Critical intellectuals with a strong group identification project their identities through a simultaneous testing and reinforcement of these marginal boundaries.

The relevance of our project to this group effort rests on a very specific reading of Debbora Battaglia's phrase "the rhetoric of self-making." We take it to refer not so much to a universal human process of ego development that has rhetorical aspects, as to the particular ideology that is summed up in the phrase "the self-made man." Nevertheless we will not analyze that kind of self-making directly. Nor will we employ an older functionalist rhetoric to discuss circumcision and head covering as techniques that a superorganic ethnic collective imposes to maintain external boundaries and internal continuity. Rather we will consider them as techniques that continue to ground a version of selfhood that is an alternative to the privatized and dehistoricized modern notion of "self-making."

The conscious embrace of these alternatives is inseparable from questions of scholarly method. Reflections contained in a recent paper by James Boon (forthcoming) are extremely helpful here. Remarking that the topic of male circumcision (let alone clitoridectomy) arouses immediate and strong unreflective opinions when discussed even in the scholarly community, Boon notes the critical difference between "empathy/distance vis-à-vis other (rather than own) circumcisions or uncircumcisions." Our examination of Jewish circumcision here, of course, concerns our "own" circumcisions. Insofar as we are speaking as Jews, this possessive pronoun implies the authoritative articulation of a common ethnic experience and reflection—something we have already tried to cast into question. Therefore we will leave open the question of whether "own" here refers to the two of us, or to all male Jews.[3]

Consistent with his plea that circumcision be treated with the same respect for cultural context that other kinds of difference enjoy, Boon emphasizes the need for a "diacritic" rather than evaluative view of circumcision (esp. 37–38). This emphasis is most appropriate, perhaps, in a study like his of "other" circumcisions/uncircumcisions. It should not be taken, however, to mean that the meanings attached to the foreskin or its absence are limited to the separation of one group from its neighbors.

Boon's paper is subtitled "An Essay amidst the History of Difficult Description," and we will similarly integrate references to the so-called past with discussions of the contemporary situation. Moving a step further, we will argue that circumcision especially raises questions about the relation between formations of chronology and of selfhood. The story of the self-made man, stripped down to its common features, starts from a zero point. It has no prehistory. It continues in linear fashion, step by step, progressively. In this version, the word *success* has lost its connotations of coming after, inheriting, taking the place of; this success, this doing well, is all about finding a high place in a capitalist hierarchy that is constantly evolving and expanding.

We suggest that this American ideal is closely linked to the Christian (and especially Protestant) notion of individual salvation, and through this to the assumption of the discrete self as existing in a uniquely defined time, such that chronology is coterminous and contingent with a sequential and progressive individual biography. The story of the self-made man, that is, begins with his birth (if he is described as having "humble beginnings," this is primarily to show that he owes nothing to anyone) and it ends with his death. The son of the self-made man cannot be self-made.

On the contrary, we will claim that a "male Jewish self"—no matter how vast the differences elided by this rubric may be—cannot be limited to such a unilinear, bounded, and progressive conception of time. The incorporation, both literal and figurative, of Jewishness as an aspect of the self implies an experience of time which is panchronic and empathetically expanded. We do not want to claim that the marks of male Jewish difference constitute essential differences from some putative white–middle-class–male–European norm. Yet they can be articulated as presenting quite rich contrasts to the rhetoric of the self-made man. The question of the link between conceptions of time and conceptions of the self is perhaps the clearest lens for examining such differences.

What we have said so far implies a more radical disjuncture than actually obtains. It suggests that an acceptance of the mark of circumcision and all of the involuntary connections that it implies place a Jewish male into a "dreamtime" or (Robert Paine's term, 1983) "totemic time" and outside the progressive time of modern self-making. Especially in contemporary middle-class America, differences in the sense of time and selfhood between most Jews and, for example, most Protestants may be negligible or impossible to determine. This attenuation of difference—symbolized, vis-à-vis the techniques of selfhood we examine here, by the prevalence in the mid-twentieth century of medical circumcision—is attributable largely to a less thoroughgoing significance of the "Jewishness" of the Jewish self. It should not let us lose sight of the distinctive modalities of Christian American selfhood.

Furthermore, our goal is not only to describe the present situation but also to recover and reevaluate earlier tropes of difference and identity. Thus, rather than dismissing the significance of marks of ethnic difference in favor of a model of voluntaristic pluralism and an open marketplace of self-invention, it is worthwhile to focus at least briefly on Jewish circumcision as a "tribal rite"—a scary one, more consequent and disturbing than ethnic foods, for instance—persisting within the heart of the Enlightened, civilized world. Greater attention to specific Jewish practices and the response to them, particularly in Christian European society, will among other things help guard us from a tendency to dismiss circumcision as merely a particular form of the general human tendency to grant greater ritual attention to males. It may also suggest surprising links between the exclusion of Jews and other forms of exclusion, especially the exclusion of women (D. Boyarin, in press). As suggested in a review of a recent collection of essays on the medieval blood libel,

> the fact that the victims were overwhelmingly male, and that in many places Jews were accused of either circumcising these youths or of needing their blood to recover that lost in circumcision, raises questions about European ideas about ethnicity and difference. The meaning of genital marking in urban Europe and concomitant ideas about male menstruation may give us greater insights into how Christians viewed Jewish genders and biologies than can be glossed by the term anti-Semitism. (White 1992, reviewing Dundes 1991)[4]

Such continuing and unresolved "questions about ethnicity and difference" were critical to the paroxysm of mid-twentieth-century Europe, the greatest symptom of which was Nazism. Some sense of the history of "circumcision" as a Christian trope, with its consequences for ideologies of embodiment, identity, and redemption, seems crucial to our ability to diagnose with any specificity the nature of that disease.

These tensions are older than Christianity, yet they are perhaps most urgently evident in the writings of Paul. Paul was virtually obsessed with circumcision. As a diacritic, the practice stood for everything that disturbed him about historical Judaism, namely its insistence on corporeality and particularly corporeal difference as a sign of real human essences.[5] The hierarchy in his work between that which is only "according to the flesh" or "in the flesh" and that which is "according to the Spirit" or "in the Spirit" refers primarily to the practice of circumcision (which is in the flesh) as opposed to the spiritual and universal practices of Christianity (notably baptism "in the Spirit"), marked by neither ethnos nor gender.

There is evidence that for Paul himself, circumcision made no difference one way or another (1 Corinthians 7:19). Yet when faced with opposition from Jewish Christians who believed that all Christians should be circumcised, Paul could write, "Look out for the dogs, look out for the evilworkers, look out for those who mutilate the flesh" (Philippians 3:2). Consideration for a moment of the fact that for a long time Europe's Others consisted of Jews, Turks, "Saracens," and "Moors"—all circumcised, of course—yields the surprising implication that un/circumcision becomes ultimately the diacritic of Christianness, while absorption of Paul's affect as in the passage just quoted renders circumcision a highly charged negative sign of un-Christianness. Othello's cry just before his suicide that thus had he done to a circumcised Turkish dog—an allusion to Paul that educated Christian audiences could not miss—makes this claim palpable.

By the Nazi period, the affect once borne by circumcision as the marker of un-Christianness became transformed into a despising of the Jewish body itself, and circumcision retained a diacritical function of exposing the Jewish body as such. While the problem of circumcision and concealment seems to have been muted in most male Jewish survivors' accounts, it is at the center of Agnieszka Holland's film *Europa, Europa,* based on the memories of Salomon Perel. Perel, a child of Polish Jews who lived in Germany before World War II, survived the war first as an enthusiastic refugee recruit of the Young Communists in the Soviet Union and then in Berlin and in the German Army by posing as an orphaned ethnic German.

Boon has also noted Salomon Perel's remarkable claim, contained in an interview with Perel which begins the film, to remember his own circumcision—something most people would consider highly unlikely for an eight-day-old infant. This exaggerated claim to remember serves both of the themes that make this film so remarkable: on the one hand the extraordinary personal talents of its protagonist, which enable him both to react promptly and to dissemble effectively; on the other hand his persistent connection to his own "rooted" Jewishness. In a subtle symmetry, the film's closing returns to Perel, and his assertion that when his own sons were born, he had them circumcised without giving it a second thought. The particular horror of the way the Nazis had turned the concealed sign on the body into a betraying mark, which made murderously clear the simultaneous historicity and pan-chronicity of identity, failed to prevent Perel from playing his part in this cyclical role of father and son.

By having his sons circumcised, at least as much as by his decision to live in Israel, Salomon Perel refused to eradicate the mark of difference that had so nearly cost him his life, to surrender retrospectively to the racialist-exclusive vision of Europe. At the same time, by writing his memoir, by agreeing to have it filmed, and by appearing in that film, he refused to divorce himself from the vision of Europe as open to historically informed difference. His resistance to the dominant European demand of amnesia is most dramatically signaled in his preternatural claim to remember his own circumcision in infancy.

Recently, however, there has appeared a somewhat widespread movement to refuse circumcision. While anticircumcision sentiments are shared by Jews and others, among Jews, they clearly have a distinctive valence. We argue that at least in part when Jews refuse to have their sons circumcised, it constitutes a refusal to perpetuate the double relation of Jews to the vision of humanity, simultaneously imperial and empathetic, that "Europe" represents. The mark of history and difference, which only in extraordinary circumstances blocks social or sexual intercourse with non-Jews, is replaced by a rhetoric of "wholeness."

Thus a recent article in the English journal *The Jewish Socialist*, written by an anonymous Jewish couple to explain their decision not to circumcise their infant son, refers to the pain of labor and breast-feeding, and continues with the following two sentences:

> After a couple of days of all that pain, I was certain that I could not take any more. I was simply not prepared to submit my miraculously perfect baby to an unnecessary medical intervention. ("Sharon and Stephen" 1992)

Obviously there is a powerful identification between the mother and the child here, so that the contemplation of even momentary, deliberately inflicted pain for the child is seen as a continuation of the mother's pain. And these are not the first Jewish parents to experience conflict at submitting their infant to this procedure; yet most Jewish parents, who identify with their children no less, still decide that internal conflict in favor of circumcision. Nor is there an explicit desire on these parents' parts to free their child of the burden of Jewish identity; both parents in this article express a concern that their child be able to enjoy being Jewish despite being uncircumcised.

This is not simply an argument about assimilation, then, although surely calling this millah (circumcision) a "medical" procedure betrays the profound involvement of these parents in a discursive paradigm that has nearly nothing to do with being Jewish at all. The distinction reminds us once again that rather than making simplistic and unidirectional claims about the weakening of group identities, we need to analyze specific techniques of difference and identity in context. What is most remarkable here is the reference to perfection, the conviction that the child as it has been born is complete and whole. This particular refusal to circumcise a child constitutes a statement of unwillingness to grant/inflict the irrevocable reminder of group identity, which in the Greco-Christian context has been and remains a confusing intermediary step between individual and generically human selfhood. The insistence on the infant's "perfection" and the denial of meaning to circumcision (calling it "an unnecessary medical intervention") may also well represent an impulse back toward a universalism and a figuration of circumcision as mutilation, which has had radical manifestations for thousands of years. The desire of these parents for an identity that will not be marked in the body, together with a yearning for a Jewish identity that will be only enjoyed, transforms the specificity of Jewish identity into the ahistoricity of an empty three-letter name, *Jew*.

The "natural" as "perfect" is not a human universal but is historically contingent—even vis-à-vis different discussions of circumcision within Judaism. In rabbinic Judaism the body is not born perfect and then "marred" to socialize it; it must in fact be symbolically "corrected." Circumcision is, as it were, an excess of creation. The following text is exemplary:

> All Israelites who are circumcised will come into Paradise, for the Holy Blessed One placed His name on Israel, in order that they might come into Paradise, and What is the name and the seal which He placed upon them? It is ShaDaY. The Shi″n [the first letter of the root], He placed in the nose, The Dale″t, He placed in the hand, and the Yo″d in the circumcision. (Tanhuma Tsav 14; cited in Wolfson 1987a, 78)

Far from being understood as a mutilation, then, or as the disturbance of a "perfection" in nature, circumcision is figured as a perfection of the human body that sanctifies it, indicating that the rabbis sensed a contingency, a disjuncture in what we are accustomed to calling "nature."[6] This sensibility resonates with the poststructuralist critique of the modern image of a dematerialized human subject confronting a detached nature that includes its own "housing" (the body) and that in itself is finished, perfect and complete.

However, not all strands of Judaism are thus consistent at all times. Maimonides "denies the implication that any natural thing could be imperfect" (Stern 1991, 36), and hence the rabbinic explanation that this could be the reason for circumcision—which is consistent with Maimonides' radical bifurcation of an idealized, apersonal Nature from an idealized Intellect. Lewis M. Barth, in his response to Stern's paper, refers to the two *mashalim* ("parables") in the Midrashic collection Bereshit Rabba that present the view of circumcision as perfecting the imperfect and cite "Walk before me and be perfect" (Genesis 17:1). He claims that "in the context of the parables, the word *tamim* . . . clearly refers to physical and not spiritual perfection" (Barth 1991, 50). But why assume that this bifurcation was operative for the rabbis? Indeed, there is every reason to assume the opposite, namely that for them there was no concept of a spiritual perfection that did not involve a perfection of the body, in the sense that they understood it, nor a physical perfection that would not imply or entail a spiritual perfection.

> It is written, "This, after my skin will have been peeled off, but from my flesh, I will see God" [Job 19:26]. Abraham said, after I circumcised myself many converts came to cleave to this sign. "But from my flesh, I will see God," for had I not done this [circumcised myself], on what account would the Holy Blessed One have appeared to me? "And the Lord appeared to him." (Genesis Rabbah 48:1; cited in Theodore and Hanoch 1965, 479)

In other texts, the foreskin is explicitly called a blemish and one, moreover, that renders the person in some sense ugly. God would not want to have spiritual contact with a person who does not remove this ugliness (Wolfson 1987b, 196–197).

> And thus it says, "Moses said: This is the thing which the Lord has commanded that you do, in order that the Glory of the Lord may appear to you" [Lev. 9:6]. What was "this thing"? He told them about circumcision, for it says, "This is the thing which caused Joshua to perform circumcision" [Josh. 5:4].
>
> "Which God commanded Abraham to do" [Lev. 9:6]. It may be compared to a shopkeeper who has a friend who is a priest. He had something unclean in his house, and he wanted to bring the priest into the house. The priest said to him: If you want me to go into your house, listen to me and remove that unclean thing from your house. When the shopkeeper knew that there was no unclean thing there, he went and brought the priest into his house. Similarly, the Holy, Blessed One, when He wanted to appear to Abraham, His beloved, the foreskin was appended to him. When he circumcised himself, immediately, He was revealed, as it says, "On that very day Abraham was circumcised" [Gen. 17:26], and immediately afterward "The Lord appeared to him" [Gen. 18:1]. (Numbers Rabbah 12:10; cited in Hadarshan 1960, D. Boyarin's translation)

For the Rabbis, as we see here, there is no disjuncture between the physical perfection of being circumcised and that *summum bonum* of the spiritual life, seeing God. This, then, is the context in which the conclusion of this text must be understood as well:

> Therefore, Moses said to them, God commanded Abraham, your father, to perform circumcision when He wished to appear to him. So in your case, whoever is uncircumcised, let him go out and circumcise himself, "that the Glory of the Lord may appear to you" [Lev. 9:6]. Thus Solomon said, "O Daughters of Zion, go forth and gaze upon King Solomon," the King who desires those who are perfect, as it is written, "Walk before Me and be perfect" [Gen. 17:1], for the foreskin is a blemish upon the body. (Numbers Rabbah 12:10; cited in Hadarshan 1960, D. Boyarin's translation)

The first "perfect" in this quotation is a pun on the name Solomon; Solomon is taken here to be God himself, while the daughters of Zion are the circumcised males of Israel. The second "perfect" is the word at issue in the Stern–Barth discussion, and it clearly means both physical perfection in the sense of the removal of the "blemish" of the foreskin as well as the spiritual perfection implied by erotic connection with God. It is precisely this lack of a breach between the physical and the spiritual that was misunderstood in post-Pauline Western culture and even in medieval Judaism from the incursion of Platonic philosophizing on. In other words, both contemporary commentators (Stern and Barth, along with virtually all postmedieval commentators on Judaism) are complicit with Maimonides in a dualistic ontology that fails to recognize rabbinic materialist monotheism.[7]

Yet materialist monotheism does not in itself explain why the rabbis chose this particular defense of circumcision. In fact, the very insistence on the foreskin as blemish is historically a response to the charge that Jews mutilate their infants. This is precisely the same sensibility that we find reccuring today, along with attacks on the very notion of prophylactic circumcision and a new fashion for piercing various body parts! Ideas of bodily perfection and imperfection, of what is counted as mutilation and what as adornment, are conditioned by the politics of identity. In the case of the rabbis (who apparently represented a *minority* of the Jews of their time), as in so many other cases, the pathos arises from the pressure on the smaller group to surrender its identity to the larger and more powerful one, and from the internal urgency to resist.

II

In a revealing way, then, the debates over distinctive bodily markings in late antiquity echo in debates going on in the time that some refer to as late modernity. To misappropriate a term from poststructuralist theory, the foreskin may be seen as one kind of "supplement," the removal of which, over generations for thousands of years, makes the male Jewish self. The tradition of covering the head is a historically variable supplement that when added helps make the male Jewish self in a different way.

In different chronotopes, these two kinds of sign have varied considerably in their significance. The head covering is much more recent as a specifically Jewish practice, although of course Jewish men have in many times and places worn the same kinds of head coverings others living around them have worn. From the "biblical" age until this century, circumcision has generally been much more effective as a distinguishing mark of the male Jew. A quick census of attendees at an academic convention in America at present, however, will reveal that most males—religious Jews, nonreligious Jews, and non-Jews—are circumcised, while virtually everyone will readily identify a man covering his head as an Orthodox Jew.

To some degree, the extent to which these two marks are matters of personal choice also varies historically and socially. One's "own" circumcision can be taken as given,[8] a point we will develop below. The freedom to decide whether or not to have a Jewish child circumcised, as we have just documented, seems at present to be growing. The head covering, on the other hand, is today virtually mandatory for Jewish males—but only if they want to be accepted as bona fide members of Orthodox Jewish communities. One of us understands his head covering more as a public mark of Jewishness than as conformity to Orthodox custom.

Although the precise history of such shifts is not to the point here, it was necessary to indicate that the two marks are themselves bound up in history. Thus, for example, any attempt to determine the meanings of Jewish circumcision at present in America cannot be limited to biblical references or rabbinic homiletics, but must take into account that circumcision is quite common among non-Jews and that anti-Semitism, while present, is relatively muted.

Sensitivity to historical variations in the markings of ethnic difference is a necessary resource for an effective debate over their contemporary functions and their fate. A recent prescription for critical thinking about subjecthood by the political theorist William Connolly offers a brace of criteria against which to measure the effects of the male Jewish diacritics we are examining:

> [Thought] may also treat historical variations in forms of selfhood, normality, and otherness as signs of the element of contrivance and contingency in each historically hegemonic formation, thereby multiplying sites at which the issues of freedom and unfreedom can be posed in late-modern life: the time of late modernity itself (as a system of interdependencies without a collectively organized agent), the state (as a center of collective agency and social discipline), the normalized self (as the center of individual agency and self-discipline), the external other produced by this standard of normality, and that in the self which resists normalization (the internal other). Each of these becomes a potential site of freedom and constraint. (1991, 35)

Connolly's prescription is at once extremely abstract and remarkably inclusive. The balance of this chapter will constitute a response to the five considerations Connolly articulates, analyzing particular instances in which circumcision and the head covering are deployed in contemporary life as sites of assertion, construction, and assault on identity.

The Time of Late Modernity Itself

As many theorists have pointed out, the particular chronological interrogation characteristic of postmodernism logically forbids our discussing it as simply another "period," analogous to the Renaissance or the Age of Reason. Rather, "time" changes, taking on distinctive characteristics in our world. As suggested in our opening remarks about circumcision as part of an alternative to the ideology of the self-made man, we operate with a concept according to which connections are not merely "with the past" along a line of time, but

rather multidirectional and located inside a chronotopic field. This understanding is consistent with the sense of recursiveness, the "drag" or hold of
the past implicit in the usages "late" or "post" modernity.

Even though most Jewish men, unlike Salomon Perel, do not recall their
own circumcision and are not expected to, the communally sanctioned and
communally observed ceremony and the mark it leaves nevertheless serve as
a reminder that the world existed before one was conscious of it, and it will
continue to exist after one's own consciousness is extinguished. The organism is bounded not only spatially, but chronologically as well; as an isolate, it
has no access to its temporal beyond. Such access is in principle unavailable
to the self-made man as well, who must frantically endeavor to create monu-
ments to himself.[9] (A well-publicized recent example is the shrine to the
career of Ross Perot located at his corporate headquarters.)

Only in a communal relationship (which of course need not be a "traditional," religious, or ethnic community) can such access, or temporal extension of the self, become possible, as Jean-Luc Nancy suggests: "Only the
community can present me my birth, and along with it the impossibility of
my reliving it, as well as the impossibility of my crossing over into my death
(Nancy 1991, 15)." It is worthwhile stressing that the unavailability to the
isolated organism of its birth and death call into question the possessive forms
"me" and "mine" here.

The insistence on a form of "selfhood" that is not plotted out on a nonre-
peating, unidirectional time line further challenges language that sees ritual
as an aspect of static "social structure." Even the more currently fashionable
term "mimesis" is inadequate as a description of the painful cut that simultaneously separates and connects.[10] For who is doing the mimesis here, and
who is being imitated? The father his father? Perhaps: When Jonah Sampson
Boyarin was circumcised, the rabbi present asked rhetorically how the acceptance of circumcision upon oneself by an eight-day-old infant could be regarded as the voluntary fulfillment of a commandment. His answer was that
the voluntary aspect of this ritual is realized later on, when the child, now
grown, permits his own child to be circumcised.

What does Rabbi Singer's homily leave then of the claim by Philippe
Lacoue-Labarthe that "there is no subject prior to imitation?" (in *La Fiction
du Politique,* summarized in Kronick 1990, 137–138). The structure of the
homily suggests that the infant is dependent not only on his father to carry
out the commandment of circumcision, but on his promised son as someone
upon whom he can then consciously perform the commandment (quite evidently another motivation of whatever preference the tradition may show for
offspring bearing penises). The subject or self does not simply imitate an

elder and thus sequentially take its place; rather, as a bundle of operated bodily signs, intentions, and actions it is distributed across a temporal weave, a textile or text.

Lacoue-Labarthe's point about the link between imitation and subjectivity also serves as a critique of the self-made man: there is no pure originality, for all subjective action has at least a moment of imitation. In the discursive tradition of rabbinic Judaism, this point is embraced. Discovering that something has already been said by someone greater is no diminution, but an enhancement, and there is an explicit redemptive value attached to citation. As the Talmud avers: "One who cites an utterance in the name of its original speaker brings redemption to the world" (Ethics of the Fathers, chap. 6).

The State

While the hegemonic nation-state form per se doubtless bears criticism in its relation to the construal of selfhood, the relation of Jews to different kinds of states differs so greatly as to make the general question almost inapplicable. Suffice it to say, before entering into specific illustrations, that whereas premodern "states" often sought to enforce Jewish distinctiveness by the prescription of distinctive clothing, modern secular states generally remain neutral or militate against such distinctions.[11] Yet the Jewish state under certain regimes has subtly encouraged the head covering as a religious-nationalist mark. Thus Menachem Begin, certainly not an Orthodox Jew, campaigned beneath a yarmulke to mark his distance from the secularist and socialist Labor Party, and also to reinforce the link between his party's longtime goal of conquering "Greater Israel," on one hand, and biblical injunctions and promises concerning the land, on the other.

Not all Jewish men in Israel or elsewhere who wear a kipa or yarmulke are sympathetic to Jewish-nationalist exclusivism. In fact, different styles of head covering may sometimes be correlated with differing political stances. The *kipa sruga*, or knitted yarmulke, is generally associated with Modern Orthodoxy and religious nationalism. Certain older styles of head covering—the round felt hat worn by certain Hasidim, the pure white knitted and pompomed yarmulke sported by others—mark the *haredim*, who proclaim that their Judaism does not require a state, or is inimical to the idea of a humanly established Jewish state. Though the styles of the head coverings that Daniel and Jonathan wear are no clue, we are two more who are opposed to Jewish state nationalism.

When religious Jews venture to communicate with Palestinians suffering Israeli occupation, they face a difficult choice. Certainly, as a matter of physical safety, the guest on the West Bank who does not want to be taken for a settler should not cover his head in public. But during the summer of 1991, when the younger of us introduced the elder to a Palestinian physician friend in Ramallah, Daniel chose to put his yarmulke back on once we were in our friend's house. When Jonathan next visited the friend, several weeks later, the physician's wife apologized for failing to introduce herself and her two young daughters to Daniel on the previous visit. "It's the kipa," she explained. "I know that your brother's a friend, but you have to understand that to us it's a frightening symbol; it makes us think the person wearing it is a murderer. My daughter was convinced that your brother had a gun." Daniel's intention was to reclaim the symbol from the racist connotations it has acquired, but at least momentarily, he was defeated. The use of the head covering as an "opening," examples of which we offer below, doesn't always work—especially not when the ethnic symbol is confused with a symbol of state power.

The same yarmulke can be an instrument of resistance to Jewish state power as well and via the same reification. During the siege of Bet-Sahour, a town near Bethlehem that undertook a tax revolt and was cut off economically and socially by the occupying forces to punish it, various Israeli peace and solidarity groups tried to get through to bring greetings. On one occasion in September of 1989, a convoy of fifty cars set out from Jerusalem. All were stopped at the check-post except for the one carrying Daniel and several other Orthodox leftists. The soldiers assumed, and we did nothing to disabuse them of their assumption, that we were settlers heading home to our colony just beyond Bet-Sahour. As a result of this tricksterism, we were able to bring back an appeal from the people of the embattled town for solidarity from Israelis of goodwill. The statement was read by Daniel with yarmulke/kipa before the television cameras of Europe and broadcast to millions of viewers throughout the Arab world, affording him fifteen minutes of fame. More important, the moment of fame his yarmulke was afforded disrupted in some small way the obviousness and univocity of its political meanings.

Circumcision remains a much more nearly ubiquitous practice among Jewish males, and it has not been co-opted by the Jewish state in the same way.[12] Indeed, a relatively early Jewish critique of circumcision suggests that while the state is masculine, circumcision represents an alternate ground of continued collective existence, one inimical to statehood. Thus Spinoza:

> The sign of circumcision is, as I think, so important, that I could persuade myself that it alone would preserve the [Jewish] nation for ~ver. Nay, I would go so far as to believe that if the foundations of their religion have not emasculated their [the Jews'] minds they may even, if occasion offers, so changeable are human affairs, raise up their empire afresh, and that God may a second time

elect them. (Geller 1993, 59; also Popkin 1990, 431, both citing the *Tractatus Theologico-Politicus*, 1951 ed., chap. 3, p. 56)

From our perspective—concerned with Jewish continuity, troubled by some Jewish practices in the light of contemporary criticism, and skeptical of the very desire for an ethnic Jewish state—this is an ambiguous and suggestive statement. Spinoza, hardly an apologist for Jewish Orthodoxy, confirms the central role of male circumcision in guaranteeing the continuity of group identity. But this form of sublimation has had a deleterious effect on the Jews' "minds"—presumably, sapping their pride and independence. For Spinoza, the kind of identity that this practice affords is a sort of sick substitute, which feminizes the [male] Jews and prevents them from erecting ("raising up") their state anew.[13] The reacquisition of a Jewish state would occur despite, not because of, the powerful practice that sustains them in exile. The talk of emasculation and erection linked to statehood is yet another example of the ways the modern state is typically figured as male, and the association of Jews with the feminine is also a common theme among both ancient rabbis and modern anti-Semites (Olender 1992). What is more interesting here is the specific way that circumcision, as a ritual that binds the collective, also cripples the capacity for autonomous masculine action (the reacquisition of a state). Yet with all this, Spinoza affirms that group identity need not be vouchsafed in a nation-state.

The Normalized Self

The sense in which Connolly uses the term "normalized" here relates primarily to an identity that is unproblematized, taken for granted, or given. In America right now, circumcision is virtually negligible as an agent for provoking reflections on history, identity, and selfhood; Spinoza's claims for its power would seem out of place in a society where a circumcised penis need not be attached to a Jew. In fact, aside from the fact that it is visible rather than hidden, the head covering—almost always a style that only Jews wear—is much more effective as a "regulator" of behavior and reminder of identity, as a social mark.

This does not yet mean that circumcision, the mark on the body, is unavailable as a ground for further reflection. If indeed we are correct, and Connolly's "normalization" can be glossed as "givenness," then in a sense the normalized self is an anomaly, as Michael Holquist suggests: "The situatedness of the self is a complicated phenomenon: it has been given the task of not being merely given" (Holquist 1989, 15). Connolly acknowledges this further on, when he refers to "that in the self which resists normalization," but whereas his language of "resistance" retains an individualist, "anti-totalitarian" residue, Holquist opts instead for a paradoxical statement of the tension between givenness (this is me) and construction (I am because making makes a "me") in selfhood.

The gap between the two marks of identity—each having its own valence vis-à-vis the tension of givenness and construction—thus becomes in some ways more acute in a period such as the twentieth century, when a large plurality of Jewish males are circumcised and yet do not actively practice Judaism or identify as religious Jews. Where there is this disjuncture between the promise implied by the prehistory of the self on one hand, and the practices (no matter how deliberately or casually settled on) of adulthood on the other, it becomes remarkably unclear what, exactly, constitutes "the normalized self": the circumcision, sign of inclusion within a limited community with its own high expectations, or the bare head, which accedes to the "normal" expectations of the broader social world.

The point here of course is not to resolve this last point in favor of assimilation or Orthodoxy, but rather to insist, following Holquist again, on the complex situation of any "identity."[14] To stereotype and freeze "the Jew" in time collapses the particular webs of relation that a practice like circumcision entails and enables, and makes it available for the sort of derision indulged in by the Latin author Petronius, who thus noted its ritual/legal centrality:

> The Jew may worship his pig-god and clamor in the ears of high heaven, but unless he also cuts back his foreskin with the knife, he shall go forth from the people and emigrate to Greek cities and shall not tremble at the fasts of Sabbath imposed by the law (Frag. 37). (Cited in Collins 1985, 163)

What Petronius elides is precisely the moment of kinship, generation, and ethnicity; for a Roman individualist, there is no difference between Jewish parents having their sons circumcised, and "the Jew" circumcising himself.[15] The moment of connection and separation is rhetorically degraded into a slavish and barbaric practice through the assumption of a singular "Jew" who is at once an ethnic stereotype and a disconnected individual. Like the modern self-made man, Petronius's Jew is perfectly and seamlessly responsible for himself; the portrait admits no prehistory.

The External Other

As we suggested above, the head covering is more significant in America for the identification of the male Jew as an external other now than circumcision, which ironically enough fails to produce an external other. In our brief discussion of the politics of identity vis-à-vis the state, we have suggested how the head covering tends to reinforce a symbolically and physically violent exclusion of the non-Jewish other from the Jewish state. It is not that most Israeli men cover their head, nor even that a "normative Israeli" public identity requires the head covering. Yet the very facts that the state is Jewish, that in this context certain types of head covering reliably indicate that their wearer is Jewish, and that only a minority of those who so cover their heads do not share the tenets of Jewish state nationalism tend to reinforce the suggestion that this place is for Jews only.

Outside the Jewish state, the head covering is also enforced as a mark of conformity to standards of belonging to various religious Jewish collectives. Jews' "external others," that is, may also be other Jews, and the head covering—generally speaking, unlike circumcision—is readily available for the drawing of this kind of distinction.

Yet such distinctions among Jews need not be pernicious. When they are explicitly articulated, they are sometimes contrasted to a more profound unity that transcends such superficial differences.

An example of such expression is contained in an anecdote told years ago to Jonathan Boyarin by Dr. Shlomo Noble. Noble had once served as an official translator in a court proceeding involving a Hasidic *rebe* who was also a diamond merchant. Noble realized that the rebe's response to a certain question might incriminate the rebe, and rather than translating it immediately, he claimed he hadn't understood the response and asked the rebe to repeat it. The rebe took the hint and rephrased his response more judiciously. Later he said to Noble, "Even though you go around bareheaded, nevertheless you have a Jewish heart." The metaphor of "heart" may seem trite to us because it seems to echo Paul's rhetoric, which tells his followers that they need only observe the biblical command to circumcise their hearts—that is, to keep the moral spirit of the law, which is "love"—and not the commandment to circumcise their flesh—here, the equivalent of the external symbol, the head covering.

Outside the Jewish state, and especially where Orthodox Jews are clearly a minority presence, the head covering can be a mark of openness and vulnerability, rather than defensiveness or exclusion vis-à-vis non-Jews. Three vignettes occasioned by Jonathan's walking around Lower Manhattan wearing a yarmulke in recent months illustrate different aspects of this claim.

1. As he walks through a Latino block late one evening, a young man sitting in front of a bodega calls out "Salaam aleikum!" three times, until the anthropologist finally turns to acknowledge the greeting and mutely waves back, too confused to reply appropriately in Arabic,

"Wa'aleikum salaam!" No less than three rather surprising ethno-graphic points may be surmised from this: first, that young Latinos have been influenced by the Islamization of urban African-American culture; second, that at least in this case, hostility toward Jews does not accompany this cultural influence; third, that for certain urban groups exposed to aspects of both Jewish and Arabic culture, the two are inter-changeable. The yarmulke on East Houston Street thus serves as a lightning rod for information that confounds stereotypes.

2. One Friday evening while Jonathan is walking to the synagogue, a man passing by him says, "L'chaim." He's fairly tall, "looks like an Indian," has a studded denim motorcycle jacket, and two black braids. He an-nounces that he's a Jewish Indian. He responds to a friendly question that he's originally from South Dakota. The anthropologist, who has had little contact with Native Americans, asks him what "people" he belongs to (a phrase learned from Tony Hillerman's books), but he has to ask again, what "tribe," before the man replies that he's a Sioux. But, he explains, as fate turned out, he was adopted by Jews and raised in Englewood Cliffs. You're a long way from home, Jonathan says sym-pathetically, but the Jewish Indian replies, "I'm the landlord. . . . This whole country belongs to me."

3. One Saturday night as Jonathan walks along East Tenth Street toward his office, four white male teenagers pass by. As they approach, one says loudly ". . . and there's too many faggots at the club." Passing on, he adds (seeing the yarmulke), "Oh, he's Jewish." Evidently something about Jonathan had clued the bully into the presumption that he should be branded a faggot. When the bully gained more information, his verbal assault on this passerby became more precise.[16] Had the yar-mulke not been present to draw the scornful designation "he's Jewish," Jonathan would not even have realized that he was being targeted as queer. The yarmulke—often taken as a symbol of conservative "family values"—here thus served as a medium of enforced empathy between different threatened marginal groups.

In other chronotopes of course—indeed, in most Jewish communities at most times—the particular way in which Jews practice circumcision has been much more significant as a means of production of self and other; in both Hebrew and Yiddish, *orel*, "uncircumcised one," is a common term for a non-Jewish male. Yet the double function of circumcision as separation and connection does not apply only to the relation between generations. Circum-

cision, the ultimate site of male Jewish difference, is also available as an opening toward the Other. In Albert Memmi's autobiographical novel *The Pillar
of Salt* (Memmi 1992 [1955]) the narrator, a Jew growing up in Tunis in the
1930s, describes being on a streetcar with various characters—a Bedouin, a
Frenchwoman, a "Mohammedan" and his two-and-a-half-year-old son, and
a Djerban grocer. The grocer begins a socially accepted form of teasing the
little boy, asking whether he's been circumcised yet, confirming that it's going to happen soon, and offering successively higher bids for his "little animal," eventually snatching at the child's groin in mock frustration and provoking the boy's real terror.

This brings the narrator back to a remembered scene in his *kouttab* school
(the North African counterpart of the East European *heder*) in which, the
teacher having briefly gone out and the class exhausting their anarchic impulse, they "felt that we needed one another and discovered that we were a
crowd . . . [and then] soon returned to ancestral traditions and decided to
play, like adults, at circumcision." They choose one of the younger boys as
the victim and carry out a mock circumcision, acting the roles of their fathers
and their future selves, until the victim bursts out crying and they all collapse
into helpless laughter. The scene from the narrator's school, in which he
simultaneously identifies with the victim and is thrilled as part of the crowd
performing the sacrifice, allows him an imaginative identification with the
Muslim child in the trolley car who, unlike a Jewish infant, will in fact be
aware of the cut that is about to be made on his body. The sentences that
link the two parts of the chapter confirm this: "Can I ever forget the Orient?
It is deeply rooted in my flesh and blood, and I need but touch my own body
to feel how I have been marked for all time by it. As though it were all a mere
matter of cultures and of elective affinities!" (1992, 169).

This is a complex statement. Memmi is postulating an Orient from a position outside it, and simultaneously identifying with it. He is asserting as a
link to fellow "Orientals" that which is usually taken (in Europe) as exclusively Jewish. Furthermore he is making a strong claim for "primal" or given
identity against modern bourgeois voluntarism. The notion of "cultures" he
derides here is one in which a culture is something one affiliates with, entirely
separate from genealogy.

The point of each of these stories is that there is no a priori reason to
assume that marks of group identity do more to isolate their bearers from
members of other groups than to multiply the possible channels of relation
between them. Such an a priori assumption is, of course, consistent with
a residual Durkheimian notion that in social life solidarity is essential and

contingent relations accidental.[17] The possibilities we have pointed to here respond instead to Connolly's call for an interrogation of the link between the production of an external Other and issues of freedom and unfreedom.

The Internal Other

Coming at the end of the list, this category—laudable for its recognition that antagonism "within" the self is to be expected and looked for, rather than regarded as pathological—hardly seems to have its own effective dynamic that would attract certain citations or anecdotes to itself. Rather, through our discussion of the simultaneous separation and connection that is performed by circumcision, and the ways in which the head covering can serve to open up unexpected empathies within the self, it has become evident that the divide between internal and external Others is only rigidly maintainable within a field of distinctions imagined spatially as between two integral and spatially discrete organisms.

Chronologically, this distinction breaks down more and more, particularly as new technologies affect the relationship between experience and consciousness. Where Salomon Perel rhetorically affects "remembering" his own circumcision, and Albert Memmi finds a form of empathetic connection to a Muslim child who is to be circumcised at the age of self-awareness, the by now much more mundane medium of videotaping enables a young Jewish child to reexperience, as it were, his own circumcision ceremony. We hasten to assure the reader that neither of us was so gauche as to film our sons' circumcision. A distant relative was kind enough to do that for one of us, however, and so we were able to witness the star of that video, by now aged three or four, calling out just before the scene of the fateful cut: "Don't do it!" In a sense that is hardly literal yet still more than allegorical, a simulacrum of one's own circumcision now can be experienced. This suggests a potential heightening of reflection as an integral aspect of self-fashioning. But, once again, there seems no point in trying to determine whether the infant depicted on the television screen is the "internal" or "external" other of the watching child.

The suggestion we are making in this section—that "resistance," rather than being concentrated in some "internal other" that is the locus of individualistic reflection, may be dispersed throughout the various other forms of self-effect that Connolly identifies—contrasts with a passage where Connolly makes clear his association of givenness with inauthenticity. There, criticizing Sartre, he refers to "self-generated pressures toward inauthenticity (pressures to treat identity as given or true rather than forged or chosen)" (1991, 103). Yet Connolly hasn't really demonstrated that treating identity as given or true is universally "inauthentic," or more to the point, necessarily repressive, since he fails to consider that certain identities are themselves, roughly speaking, "hegemonic" and others "resistant." Nor does he quite acknowledge how historically specific the ideal of treating identity as forged or chosen is.[18]

Most important for our discussion here is an assumption that remains implicit within Connolly's argument: that an ironic stance toward given identities is a modern consciousness unfamiliar to "traditional" discourses, that it is something we should and can only cultivate afresh from within ourselves. While Connolly explicitly acknowledges the embeddedness of the self and the necessity of a moment of prior givenness in selfhood, he does not see these as sources for a tolerant play of difference. Rather the compromises he offers recall the reluctant acknowledgment of human corporeality in certain strands of Christian thinking.

These assertions are not made to dismiss Connolly's lucid discussion. Rather they are intended to suggest how difficult it is to negotiate in theory the intellectual tightrope between a celebration of what he would call capital-I Identity on one hand, and a subtle recourse to the ideal of the autonomous subject on the other. Judith Butler warns that to ignore relations (of kin, and other kinds) is to reproduce the alienated modern subject: "the subject is constituted through an exclusion and differentiation, perhaps a repression, that is subsequently concealed, covered over, by the effect of autonomy. In this sense, autonomy is the logical consequence of a disavowed dependency" (1991, 157).

We have been arguing throughout this chapter that what theory discusses as the negotiation of pulls toward "individual" and "collective" selfhood, toward conscious autonomy and given relatedness, is imperfectly effected in Judaism through the double mark of the male Jew.[19] If we take the avowal of dependency in Jewish ritual as "that in the self which resists ['self-making'] normalization," then circumcison and the head covering can indeed be conceived (!) as sites for critical posing of freedom and unfreedom.

A last word remains to be written, however, for as it stands we seem to have simply striven to "vindicate" our own Identity against yet another call for reflexive self-awareness. On the contrary, this investigation itself should stand as evidence that we endorse Connolly's program of investigating the way in which our own identity is constructed. Even though we have emphasized the ways traditional signs offer the possibility of a dialogic and nonhierarchical construction of identity, we certainly agree that those signs need also to be examined in their overreaching and imperious effects. Yet we cannot agree that such a critical stance need be opposed to "the voices of strong identity," for as we claimed at the outset, such are our voices. "Weak" or

poorly informed identities can be shrilly defensive. "Strong" identities can—
it seems obvious once stated—be resilient, self-confident, and ironic. Indeed,
identities that bear within themselves the marks of their own generation are
most likely to tolerate a "generative doubt" that affords the possibility of
"non-isomorphic subjects, agents, and territories of stories unimaginable
from the vantage point of the cyclopian, self-satiated eye of the master subject" (Haraway 1991, 192). Such an alternative vantage point is potentially
afforded by the double mark of the male Jew.

NOTES

1. In revising this chapter for publication, we have chosen to retain the marks of
its original venue, including our joint appearance as brothers—an affinity both given
and chosen—on the convention podium.

2. The reliance here on a mixture of spatial and temporal metaphors that nevertheless still tend to be seen as representing separate, objective axes is dissected in J.
Boyarin 1994.

3. Gil Anidjar (forthcoming) criticizes us here for assuming that the circumcision
is performed upon what already *is* a "boy," rather than seeing the milah as a process
of boy making, as would be implied by the insight of Judith Butler that "the moment
when an infant becomes humanized is when the question, 'is it a boy or girl?' is
answered" (1990, 111).

4. The contrast between menstruation and the letting of blood in circumcision on
one hand, and the symbolic representation of the Eucharistic wine as "the blood of
Christ" on the other, is consistent with a Greco-Christian pattern in which allegorical
representation is consistently seen as superior and transcendent over literal or material
substances. The application of such hierarchies was later applied to newly colonized
peoples. The Spanish writer Sepulveda explained the native practice of cannibalism by
arguing that "such sacrifice represented a diabolic category mistake, a substitution of
a living organism, the heart, for a metaphysical entity, 'the pious and sane minds of
men.' Instead of metaphorically 'sacrificing' the latter, the Indian literally immolates
the former" (cited in Pagden 1986, 143–144). Shades here—as below in an example
drawn from *Jewish* discourse—of Paul's claim that the injunction to circumcise the
heart supersedes the injunction to circumcise the flesh.

5. D. Boyarin 1994 deals with this interpretation of Paul at length.

6. Daniel Boyarin has argued that this sanctification occurs in two ways: First of all
it renders the male Jewish body different from male non-Jewish bodies. The figural
use of "uncircumcised" as a term of reprobation of Gentiles indicates this. But also
there is evidence that circumcision feminizes the male body through the blood and
also by removing an unnecessary bit of flesh that renders that body more "male." See
D. Boyarin 1992 for the argument.

7. Stern does recognize the gap between the rabbis and Maimonides that Barth
attempts to reduce.

8. Although perhaps not irreversible. The Knoxville, Tennessee, *Metro Pulse* for
the week April 27–May 3 1992 picked this up from the San Jose *Mercury-News:*

An organization of several dozen men meets regularly in the San Francisco area to discuss ways to restore their foreskins. . . . RECAP ("Recover a Penis") members are divided as to technique between surgical reconstruction and "stretching," described by founder Wayne Griffiths as pulling loose skin over his penis and taping it in place using "Fore-balls," a device he invented, consisting of two small ball bearings that add weight to pull the skin down. Griffiths said he wore the device for up to 12 hours a day, five days a week, for a year, and that he now has enough skin to cover the head of his penis without taping. "The [sexual] feelings are sensational," he said. Said a urologist who supports the group, "They want to enhance their image whether it's in their pants or on their face. Who am I to say otherwise? No way. No way."

9. That the phrase "self-made man" is not immediately perceived as oxymoronic is another indication of the dualism that pervades hegemonic modern thinking. Of course nobody is self-made. The more obvious link between women's bodies and the making of other human beings might help to explain why we seldom hear the phrase, "self-made woman."

10. In biblical Hebrew, the verb used for making a covenant is precisely "cutting," and another famous covenant between God and Abraham is sealed by Abraham's walking between the cut halves of a sacrificed animal (Genesis 15). On the one hand, it may be entirely too convenient to insist that such symbolism reflects the awareness that such covenants always entail a diminution, a sort of violence to what we fondly take to be the autonomous self. On the other hand, the puzzlement this symbolism evokes among contemporary readers of the Bible suggests that, even though we say "cut a deal," we would much prefer not to be cut by the deals we make. See also Schwartz 1992.

11. Thus there have been a series of lawsuits over the issues of Orthodox Jewish men being permitted to wear beards or to cover their heads while serving in the U.S. military. A more spectacular recent example is the case of the two young Muslim girls from North African families who insisted on veiling their faces when they went to public school. The French state strongly resisted and then eventually relented, in the face of massive Muslim agitation. In that case the major French Jewish organizations actively sided with the Muslims.

12. Given, however, the nature of ideological state apparatuses and the recent well-publicized circumcisions of adult immigrants from the former Soviet Union, this claim may require modification.

13. For discussion of the association between circumcision and castration, see Shell 1988, 216 n. 61, and references there.

14. This common term is set off in quotation marks here because it bears a prejudicial charge against ambiguity.

15. Compare the detemporalized and radically individualist critique of culture by Walter Benn Michaels (1992) and our response to Michaels, which forms part of our essay "Generation: Diaspora and the Ground of Jewish Identity" (D. Boyarin and J. Boyarin 1993).

16. The gay community in New York City has recently organized self-defense patrols to counter a dramatic increase in antigay street violence. Not until I read a street poster for a march against antigay violence while writing a draft of this chapter did I realize that I had also risked physical violence on the street that night.

17. The strategy of separating the "essential" from the "accidental" is employed in Western thinking from Aristotle to Hegel.

18. Although, to be fair, Connolly is careful not to advance his ideal as an inevitable or necessary one:

> Such a counter-doctrine cannot advance itself as a singular truth. It must not, for instance, strive to purge doctrines that rest upon faith in a true identity or a particular god. It seeks, instead, to give voice to a perspective with a reverence of its own and to limit the extent to which the voices of strong identity can define the terms through which alter-identities are recognized and responsibility is distributed. It seeks to politicize identity and responsibility. (118)

19. Imperfectly not only since we have already rejected perfection as a criterion, but more specifically because the mark of circumcision is itself "concealed, covered over" in public.

REFERENCES

Anidjar, Gil. Forthcoming. "J'Oublie: A Jew Bleeds: About Circumcision." In *Jews and Other Differences,* edited by Jonathan Boyarin and Daniel Boyarin. Minneapolis: University of Minnesota Press.

Barth, Lewis M. 1991. "Circumcision and the Unity of God: A Comment on Stern." *Sevara* 2:49–51.

Benjamin, Walter. 1969. "Theses on the Philosophy of History." In *Illuminations,* edited by Hannah Arendt, translated by Harry Zohn, 253–264. New York: Schocken.

Boon, James. Forthcoming. "Circumscribing Circumcision/Uncircumcision: An Essay amidst the History of Difficult Description." In *Implicit Ethnographies,* edited by Stuart Schwartz. New York: Cambridge University Press.

Boyarin, Daniel. 1992. " 'This We Know to Be the Carnal Israel': Circumcision and the Erotic Life of God and Israel." *Critical Inquiry* 18(Spring):474–506.

———. 1994. *A Radical Jew: Paul and the Politics of Identity.* Berkeley, Los Angeles, London: University of California Press.

———. In press. "Allegoresis against Difference; Or, the Metalinguistic Origins of the Universal Subject." *Paragraph.*

Boyarin, Daniel, and Jonathan Boyarin. 1993. "Diaspora: Generation and the Ground of Jewish Identity." *Critical Inquiry* 19(Summer):693–725.

Boyarin, Jonathan. 1992. *Storm from Paradise: The Politics of Jewish Memory.* Minneapolis: University of Minnesota Press.

Boyarin, Jonathan, ed. 1994. *Space, Time, and the Politics of Memory.* Minneapolis: University of Minnesota Press.

Butler, Judith. 1990. *Gender Trouble: Feminism and the Subversion of Identity.* New York: Routledge.

———. 1991. "Contingent Foundations: Feminism and the Question of 'Postmodernism.' " *Praxis International* 11:150–165.

Collins, John J. 1985. "A Symbol of Otherness: Circumcision and Salvation in the First Century." In *"To See Ourselves as Others See Us": Christians, Jews, "Others" in Late Antiquity,* edited by Jacob Neusner and Ernest S. Frerichs, 163–186. Scholars Press Studies in the Humanities. Chico, Calif.: Scholars Press.

Connolly, William E. 1991. *Identity/Difference: Democratic Negotiations of Political Paradox.* Ithaca, N.Y.: Cornell University Press.

Dundes, Alan, ed. 1991. *The Blood Libel Legend: A Casebook in Anti-Semitic Folklore.* Madison: University of Wisconsin Press.

Fabian, Johannes. 1983. *Time and the Other.* New York: Columbia University Press.

Geller, Jay. 1993. "A Paleontological View of Freud's Study of Religion: Unearthing the *Leitfossil* Circumcision." *Modern Judaism* 13:49–70.

Hadarshan, Shim'on. 1960. *Numbers Rabbah.* Tel Aviv: Moriah.

Haraway, Donna J. 1991. *Simians, Cyborgs, and Women: The Reinvention of Nature.* New York: Routledge.

Holquist, Michael. 1989. "From Body-Talk to Biography: The Chronobiological Bases of Narrative." *The Yale Journal of Criticism* 3(Fall):1–37.

Kronick, Joseph G. 1990. "Dr. Heidegger's Experiment." *Boundary 2* 17(Fall):116–153.

Lustick, Ian. 1988. *For the Land and the Lord: Jewish Fundamentalism in Israel.* New York: Council on Foreign Relations.

Memmi, Albert. 1992 [1955]. *The Pillar of Salt.* Boston: Beacon Press.

Michaels, Walter Benn. 1992. "Race into Culture: A Critical Genealogy of Cultural Identity." *Critical Inquiry* 18(Summer):655–686.

Nancy, Jean-Luc. 1991. *The Inoperative Community.* Minneapolis: University of Minnesota Press.

Olender, Maurice. 1992. *The Languages of Paradise: Race, Religion, and Philology in the Nineteenth Century.* Translated by Arthur Goldhammer. Cambridge: Harvard University Press.

Pagden, Anthony. 1986. *The Fall of Natural Man.* New York: Columbia University Press.

Paine, Robert. 1983. "Israel and Totemic Time?" *Royal Anthropological Institute Newsletter* 59.

Popkin, Richard. 1990. "Medicine, Racism, Anti-Semitism: A Dimension of Enlightenment Culture." In *The Languages of Psyche: Mind and Body in Enlightenment Thought,* edited by G. B. Rousseau, 405–442. Berkeley, Los Angeles, Oxford: University of California Press.

Ratzel, Friedrich. 1898. *The History of Mankind, Vol. 3.* London and New York: Macmillan.

Schwartz, Regina M. 1992. "Nations and Nationalism: Adultery in the House of David." *Critical Inquiry* 19(Autumn):131–150.

"Sharon and Stephen." 1992. "A Considered Decision." *The Jewish Socialist* 26(June–August):19.

Shell, Marc. 1988. *The End of Kinship: Shakespeare, Incest, and the Religious Orders.* Stanford, Calif.: Stanford University Press.

Stern, Josef. 1991. "Maimonides' Parable of Circumcision." *Sevara* 2:35–48.

Theodor, Jehuda, and Albeck Hanoch, eds. 1965. *Genesis Rabbah.* Jerusalem: Wahrmann.

von Rad, Gerhard. 1962. *Old Testament Theology.* Vol. 1. *The Theology of Israel's Historical Traditions.* Translated by D. M. G. Stalker. New York: Harper and Row.

White, Luise. 1992. Review of *Blood Libel Legend,* ed. Alan Dundes. *Times Literary Supplement,* May 15, p. 23.

Wolfson, Elliot R. 1987a. "Circumcision and the Divine Name: A Study in the Transmission of Esoteric Doctrine." *Jewish Quarterly Review* 78(July–October):77–112.

———. 1987b. "Circumcision, Vision of God, and Textual Interpretation: From Midrashic Trope to Mystical Symbol." *History of Religions* 27(November):189–215.

THREE

On Eccentricity

George E. Marcus

Eccentricity has always abounded when and where strength of character has abounded.

—JOHN STUART MILL

Writing this chapter has provided me with an opportunity to pull together two major strands of argument in a recently completed study of mature American dynastic families and fortunes, *Lives in Trust* (1992), so as to think more about a lingering puzzle that I frequently encountered in this milieu: that of eccentric behavior and identity. Eccentricity has indeed been a particularly difficult social psychological category to address systematically and analytically in social science writing, except to simply describe the behaviors and biographies of famous eccentrics. Here, I want to develop some theoretical ideas about eccentricity relevant to the particular locus of my work: contemporary dynasties in which persons are formed by being both subjects and objects of great power, wealth, and sometimes, celebrity.

One main line of argument in my research had to do with the extreme salience among heirs to inherited wealth of the mediated nature of their lives. To a greater extent and awareness than most persons in modern (postmodern?) society, the identities of the extremely wealthy are multiply authored by agents and agencies over which they have variant and often limited control. Perhaps the key example is the management of individual shares of ancestral wealth through a complex division of labor among experts such as lawyers, bankers, investment consultants, and so on—fiduciaries, in short—which in turn amounts to the construction over time of a doubled, parallel self of an heir that might be experienced by him or her as something akin to a doppelganger, or familiar, produced by a mostly hidden world of expertise. Other kinds of doubled selves are authored by journalists, philanthropic clients, corporate executives, public relations and media consultants, and even scholars like me. An heir's relation or response to his or her keen awareness of these multiply authored, doubled, parallel selves in different vaguely understood spheres of production will constitute one important frame for the understanding of eccentricity in contexts of great power, wealth, and celebrity.

The second line of argument, deriving from a special case of the first, concerns the question of the efficacy of ancestral (often patriarchal) authority within the family of heirs/descendants itself despite modern conditions of widespread skepticism about and resistance to anything like the personal exercise of patriarchal upper-class authority by a dynastic leader. This kind of authoritative leadership has often devolved by the third generation upon the hidden world, to which I referred, constituted by the division of expert labor. Still, in many dynasties, ancestral figures continue to exert considerable, and particularly intimate, power in the lives of even the most resistant and skeptical descendants. This is the kind of invisible ancestral world of authority among traditional peoples that anthropologists are accustomed to studying, but here, instead, is a world of authority among capitalist dynasts without the aid of sacred rituals, shamans, or supporting cultural articulations of belief in such authority. How, then, does the ancestor otherwise have efficacy among wealth-bound moderns?

The answer I posed was framed in terms of postulating a deeply embedded, recurrent, and pervasive discourse of distinction and socialization within descendant families that was concerned *primarily* with both shaping and evaluating the personhood of family members, especially in relations across generations. Of course, this might be seen as the hyperdevelopment of the way that a collective ideology of its own special peculiarity or distinction is inculcated in the individuals of any family. In dynastic families, however, ancestral figures constitute a standard of "character" that is especially salient in the assessment of persons, by parents of children, by siblings of each other, and ultimately by children of parents. Besides distinctive notions of family character on which the distinction or honor of a family rests, descendants also often harbor distinctive ideas or family theories of how ancestral personhood is transmitted and distributed. These are often a mix of something like Frazerian mimetic theories of magic and eugenic notions.

In any case, my interest in the efficacy of ancestral authority under adverse modern conditions came to rest on ideologies of distinction, and particularly on how dynasts are constituted as distinctive persons. The cohort of mature dynasties with which I was concerned are now in their third to fifth generations and originated in the later nineteenth century through the founding fortunes accumulated by entrepreneurial capitalists who accomplished the economic integration of American society. In their contemporary period of maturity, distinctive personhood seems to rest now as much upon an ambivalently constructed valorization of eccentricity as upon models of obviously virtuous and positive character that particular families produced generation after generation among their members. This fetishization, so to speak, of eccentricity within certain families I studied is what stimulated me to think more analytically about the phenomenon of eccentricity itself in dynastic contexts, which is the main concern of this chapter.

A digression is useful here to give a specific historical context to the theoretical speculations of this chapter. It concerns heightened, self-conscious fascination with eccentricity as a marked collective cultural formation among upper classes in American society at certain junctures. Unfortunately, such a history has yet to be written (but see Hall 1982), so in presenting this brief portrait, I have relied largely on discussion with Peter Dobkin Hall, my collaborator on *Lives in Trust* and incomparable historian of New England upper classes and their role in shaping national institutions.

Character discourse, as diffusely permeating relations within the upper-class families of Boston, was not only a key means of socializing children to the already strong structures of class authority in the family and supporting institutions (colleges, charities, professions) but also the exemplary model of virtuous personhood toward which aspiring entrants to elite life should strive. Such aspirants included the post–Civil War cohort of entrepreneurial capitalists, based in growing urban centers across the United States, who eventually succeeded in cultural status and economic power the colonial gentry elites of New England. This is the cohort with whose fourth- to fifth-generation descendants I was mainly concerned in my research. But just as these later metropolitan elites were beginning to form up in the early nineteenth century, Hall suggests, the virtuous notion of character began to shift from meaning those attributes which make an individual or trait distinctive to meaning the bundle of behavioral attributes that make an individual dependable or reliable. Thus, while character, as an exclusive quality, "the right stuff," so to speak, retained this mystique for a time in the context of socialization to authority within upper-class families, it lost its precise prestigious hold over society at large and rising classes within it. Character discourse in the original sense, then, involuted upon the internal dynamics of upper-class families themselves. Character as dependability now fit within the work discipline of capitalist expansion, and lost its particular, exclusive aristocratic edge.

There is no doubt that the New England gentry explicitly felt themselves in decline at a number of points during the long process of their replacement by new elites—particularly during the 1840s and 1850s, and again at the turn of the nineteenth century. It was during these times that there was a marked collective preoccupation with eccentricities among themselves—when eccentricity became a theme of literature, social commentary, autobiography, and family memoir produced by this class. At such times, I would argue, eccentricity served as both a preoccupation with decline and the rather perverse expression of a final essence of class exclusivity and honor.

The national upper class that finally succeeded the cultural dominance of the old New England gentry classes into the twentieth century was to a certain extent a product of the educational institutions and cultural models of class institutions of this originary (and only) American aristocracy. Within the dynastic families of this class, based on the amassing of great business fortunes, there was an attempt to reinstantiate a character discourse of the exclusive type for the purposes of inculcating authority among descendants by controlling their persons, so to speak, by evaluations according to models of distinctive, virtuous family character. However, the social tide was against this as an efficient technique of class solidarity, since elite formation in the increasingly diverse United States had long since escaped the narrow channels of prestige defined by Boston Brahmins, Philadelphia gentlemen, and New York gentry. With the decline of these aristocrats, there was no longer the class institutional support for patriarchal authority within dynastic families. Socialization to dynastic authority (but not necessarily class authority) of children by the subtle evaluation and shaping of their persons according to distinctive standards of very specific family character has indeed remained efficacious. However, the preoccupation with eccentricity—making a collective family fetish of it from the labeling and marking of particular family members across generations as eccentrics—has remained a means, alternative to character, of creating a strong family ideology among descendants in a mature dynasty that seems to be breaking up, except for the arrangements of sharing wealth that continue to tie individuals together. While I have not noted among "old wealth" upper classes of the twentieth century a repeat of the moments of collective class preoccupation with eccentricity that marked periods of self-perceived decline among the old gentry elite during the nineteenth century, categorically eccentric behavior within individual family histories has remained a variable but widespread component of a mature dynasty's collective self-awareness, a salient counterpoint to the usual effort to establish intimate family identification in persons by distinctive evaluation of character. While ambivalently discussed and focused upon, eccentricity also serves to mark distinction and honor, when there are few other resources with which to do so.

In the history of American upper classes and dynastic families, then, eccentricity is far from being obviously deviant, nonconformist behavior. Rather, it is the untamed or undomesticated side of positively valorized "character."

It is what replaces this character discourse of a particular class or individual dynasty in decline as a sort of last bulwark of resentful privilege, an indulgence imposed upon the masses (or simply, others) as a last resort in the desire for distinction. Eccentricity here is inflected with exclusivity and excess—the unself-conscious characteristics of personhood among some of its members that a whole class or a single dynasty self-consciously draws upon to define its final excruciating, but exclusive, predicament. Finally, such a class or dynasty, by becoming preoccupied with distinctive eccentricity among its members and elevating this eccentricity to an emblem of collective condition, where a highly influential standard of character once held, makes society, which no longer recognizes it in any mystified way, now suffer its excesses.

THE STRANGENESS OF ECCENTRICITY, OR THE LIMITING CONDITIONS OF AN INTRACTABLE CATEGORY

Now I attempt to define the distinctive features of the concept of eccentricity as a set of behaviors and an identity. This must needs be an exercise of specifying as much what eccentricity is *not* as what it is, since it is clearly a category that hovers between very positive and negative associations. For example, the defining nonconformism of eccentricity might be associated with the worthless "drunkard and fool" epithet that is a judgment always awaiting failures in dynastic families, or it might be associated with various kinds of clinically assessed mental illness, or it might, alternatively, be associated with the gift of originality and genius. As I noted, most studies of eccentrics have simply occupied themselves with marveling at the occult spectacle of eccentricity through providing biographical descriptions of famous eccentrics. In the following discussions of the distinctive features of eccentrics, I steer between aspects that seem to capture a defining essence for eccentricity—but any one of which singly fails to do so—and I will primarily be concerned with the ambiguities in how the category itself gets constructed.

Eccentricity by definition and situation is *not* clinical, or within the realm of neurosis and pathology, even though it is often discussed and understood as if it were mental illness. The one monographic study that I found on eccentricity (Weeks and Ward 1988) indeed approached eccentric behavior in terms of formal protocols of personality disorder. While descriptively useful, it violates a boundary that sustains eccentric behavior in embedded social life distinct from mental illness. In fact, well-known eccentrics may move into medical or therapeutic treatment, but from an ethnographic perspective, it is useful to try to understand eccentricity this side of clinical observation, so to speak, existing as a fully viable form of life in society, a feature that indeed distinguishes it as eccentricity, as *not* mental illness.

In an interesting recent book (1992), Louis Sass attempts to link historic theories of madness to the aesthetics of high modernism. His linking argument is that both modernism and madness are produced through and in selves that "suffer" from hyper-self-awareness, even to the sensation or effect of a loss of self. Eccentrics, I would argue, in contrast, exhibit very little self-awareness or self-consciousness in the sense of introspection. Rather, they are hyperaware that their selves are being constructed elsewhere by other agencies, that they are keenly aware of their selves being multiply authored. Thus, eccentricity arises not so much from an extreme awareness of self, but from an extreme awareness of how one's self is being constructed by other agencies. This key feature of eccentricity recalls the distinctive condition of doubling or mediation in self-construction that characterizes heirs to great wealth, which I mentioned in the introduction to this chapter, and which will be elaborated in terms of the notion of mimesis in a following section. The point, here, is that eccentrics do not produce interesting introspective discourses about the self, or their own behavior and identity. They are more likely to engage with and comment upon the production of their selves by other agencies, and this engagement is less likely to be in the form of literal discourse than in the form of the behaviors, performances, and habits that constitute eccentricity itself.

A corollary to this last feature is that "eccentric" is rarely if ever a term of self-reference but is a label of social judgment of a particular person's behavior. One could thus easily and conveniently focus on eccentricity as a matter of social construction, more in the eye of the beholder than in the mind of the eccentric person, who, as I have noted, is distinctively not self-aware enough to provide an interesting account of his or her own eccentricity as a personal matter. From the perspective of the social judgment and attribution of eccentricity to particular persons, especially of great wealth, power, or celebrity, eccentricity is often associated with the distortion effect or excess associated with the bearing of great wealth or the exercise of great power. That is, merely bearing great wealth or exercising great power is quite exotic in the imaginations of most people; unless the powerful or wealthy person works at seeming common, he or she is vulnerable to seeming eccentric merely by the condition of excess in which he or she is embedded.

Eccentricity is thus constitutive of received myths of power and wealth. It is simply the "distortion effect" of the wielding of great power, the possessing of great wealth, or even of the experiencing of fame upon the person, rather than an intrinsic, psychological characteristic of the person (which indeed is the emphasis of the therapeutic/pathological version and context of eccentricity). This means that there is a fundamental ambiguity in the attribution of eccentricity in a person's wielding of great power: a person might be eccentric in relation to the doubling/mimetic situation that I will discuss further (what might be termed the "doppelganger effect," in distinction to the "distortion effect"), or more often, eccentricity is constructed from a social judgment or perception whereby the wielding of great power or bearing of great wealth as an activity of excess by a person lends itself to the labeling of that person as eccentric.

The judgment by society of rich, powerful, or famous eccentrics is bound to be tinged with class resentments. When a standard of positively valued character—the so-called role model of aspiration for socially mobile others—declines and eccentric excess takes its place, such eccentricity, while being the last bulwark of distinctive nonconformity for the family that comes to revel in it as their own predicament, becomes associated by a larger public with a certain aggressive superiority that the rich and powerful as eccentrics are able to impose and that stands for a presumed entitlement to bend the environments over which they have control toward indulging their nonconformist excesses. The eccentric rich, thus, have the capacity to normalize the institutions and personnel they control in line with what others judge as their peculiarities. Therefore the public associates a certain meanness and injustice with wealthy eccentricity.

There is thus always an aspect of class resentment or desire associated with eccentricity, even when it is identified and labeled among persons of middle- or lower-class (working-class) standing, as it is on a widespread basis in English society. In such an explicitly class-bound society as England, the bemused nonconformities of working-class and middle-class eccentrics have something of the privilege and pretension of aristocracy—sort of an existential claim, when material conditions do not permit it, of the sort of distinction of excess that is normally indulged by the powerful and the wealthy. The same is perhaps true of American society, but being less explicitly class-bound in its social thought, eccentricity is predominantly associated with the lavishly powerful, wealthy, and famous, and when it is not, and it also escapes clinical assessment as mental illness, its class associations are much more muted and masked.

Perhaps the relevant analogy here is: as the (class-privileged) dilettante is to the hard-working serious professional, so eccentricity is to character. The defining feature of eccentricity in this regard is the willingness of people, the public, to indulge it, and even respect it. This willingness affords to the one labeled an eccentric—even of modest middle-class or working-class standing—a certain deference that is usually reserved for those who are clearly able to impose their eccentricity, which in upper-class history is a peculiar deformation of character of a class in decline.

Finally, referring back to the earlier key point about the lack of personal self-awareness in eccentrics, individuals who have been labeled and focused upon as eccentric seem to be distinguished by obsessions and construction of fetishes. While there are elaborate psychological theories about both obsession and fetishism that ground these in notions of how personality is formed, I prefer to focus on the specifically microsocial conditions that might give a context to eccentric obsession. This of course does not exclude the equal importance of purely psychological dynamics. Indeed, eccentric obsessions and fetishes are the medium by which a person deals with the extreme awareness of the doublings and the multiple authorship of his or her self by other agencies elsewhere. In this speculation, the older meanings of obsession and fetishism (investment by evil spirits and ritualistic orientation toward objects of enchantment) will be more relevant than their domesticated uses in clinical judgments and theories about personality disorder. They may indeed mark personality disorders in contexts of eccentricity, but because eccentricity in its own bounding as a concept is distinct from pathology, I prefer to consider the obsessions and fetishes that characterize eccentric behavior socially and relationally, and this is what brings us back to the older, "primitivist" associations of the terms.

The following, then, are some of the specific kinds of behaviors that constitute lives that have been characterized as eccentric, again with the dynastic context of great wealth in mind.

1. In the context of great wealth, extreme hoarding behavior, or miserliness, and/or extreme extravagance in expenditure. An example is the apocryphal story of the Rockefeller who would not spare a dime for a phone call. Another is the Hearst castle. A third is the revelation of the impoverished conditions in which Howard Hughes lived.

2. Extreme privacy or withdrawal from most social contacts, as in the case, again, of Howard Hughes, or J. D. Salinger, or Greta Garbo.

3. Fear of infection, disease, or subversion (the form of eccentricity closest to the clinical definition of paranoia), resulting in rituals of either extreme cleanliness, or the opposite, or in a variety of body and food obsessions.

4. Inversions of commonsense habits, gender identifications, and dress. These deal with nonconformism in the presentation of self socially and are most likely to be judged as self-conscious strategies in which there is an intention to be eccentric.

Indeed when eccentricity becomes the collective emblem of distinctive identity among a social class or a mature dynasty in decline, peculiarities of behavior can become hypostatized and self-conscious as a perverse
form of privilege, but I would argue that the whole range of observed eccentric behaviors in their individual manifestations, as opposed to being seized
upon as the emblem of class or family ideology, are obsessions and fetishes
that have much more to do with the "mimetic faculty," as Walter Benjamin
termed it and Michael Taussig has recently made much of (1992a, 1992b).

MIMESIS, OR THE OCCULT, EXOTIC SENSE OF ECCENTRICITY

*In Some Way or Another One Can Protect Oneself from Evil Spirits by
Portraying Them*

—MICHAEL TAUSSIG

*The story of my family! The story of my family in my town: I didn't think about
it; but it was in me, this story, for the others; I was one, the last of this family;
and I had in me, in my body, its imprint and in countless habits of action and
thought, that I had never considered, though the others recognized them clearly
in me, in my way of walking, laughing, greeting. I believed myself a man in
life, an ordinary man, who lived day by day a basically idle existence, however
full of curious errant thoughts; no, no, no, I could be an ordinary man for
myself, but not for the others; for the others I had many summary features,
which I hadn't made or given to myself and to which I have never paid any
attention; and my belief that I was an ordinary man, I mean even my idleness,
which I believed truly mine, was not mine for the others; it had been given me
by my father, it derived from my father's wealth; and it was a fierce idleness,
because of my father.*

—LUIGI PIRANDELLO

The varieties of behavior defining eccentricities enumerated above are, in
contexts of descent within family/fortune complexes of inherited wealth,
manifestations of obsessions and fetishes that define the relationship of heirs
to the agencies that produce their doubles. Recall the defining feature of the
eccentric as the person whose own sense of self is most strongly developed as
a keen awareness that his or her self is doubled and multiply authored.

In writing about this feature of the construction of dynastic authority, I
drew upon an extended analogy with life in traditional society, particularly as
described in the ethnography of the Kaluli people of New Guinea by Edward
and Bambi Schieffelin and Steven Feld (see Marcus 1992, chap. 5). The foundation of cultural order among the Kaluli rests on the positing of an unseen
world that intimately parallels the happenings of everyday life. Phenomeno-
logically, this unseen world is experienced through an aesthetic of sounds
and sounding, as Steve Feld has recounted. In the richly diverse sounds of

the forest, the unseen world is always present for the Kaluli. While known by
the Kaluli in everyday life in an episodic, commonsensical, and fragmented
way, the unseen world is systematically imagined in ritual through mediums
who, roughly like an ethnographer, have been to this other world and have
seen what ordinary people can hear only traces of in the sounds of the forest.

Communication with the unseen world is primarily mimetic rather than
discursive. That is, it depends on performance and the senses—a making contact through imitating, an embodying—rather than on discourse. Copying
what is seen in vision or heard as sounds makes the other world present and
gives humans some control over their doubles in an otherwise inaccessible
sphere. I argued that the experience of sharing in a great concentration of
inherited, abstract wealth is similar to the Kaluli's sensing of an unseen world
that parallels theirs in which actions in either world have direct consequences
for the other. Here I want to argue that, at least for eccentric heirs to great
wealth, the mode of relationship or communication between themselves and
the unseen world of wealth production and management is, as for the Kaluli,
mimetic rather than discursive. In this sense, eccentric obsessions and fetishes
are primarily mimetic concerns.

Mimesis itself has been the recent subject of interesting theoretical elabo-
ration by Michael Taussig (1992a, 1992b), who in turn has been inspired by
Walter Benjamin and his alternative to purely language-based approaches to
the understanding of modern life. The critical notion in Benjamin on which
Taussig meditates (1992a, 23) is the idea of "the radical displacement of
self in sentience—taking one outside oneself. No proposition could be more
fundamental to understanding the visceral bond connecting perceiver to perceived [and connecting eccentric heir to wealth, I would interject] in the
operation of mimesis," says Taussig. The so-called mimetic faculty, operating
through obsessive habit, takes the eccentric heir into the alterity of hidden
worlds where wealth is produced in the operation of economics and account-
ing while his or her self is doubled as literally an "account" of economic
value.

In place of a discourse of the self, then, or the social construction of the
self, to which ethnographers have generally looked as the source of data on
the basis of which to theorize the self as a cultural phenomenon, we have
mimesis—a thoroughly performative, sensorial, and unself-conscious response to the social conditions that define one's selfhood—conditions that
involve hidden or only partially understood parallel worlds of agency. The
obsessions and fetishism that constitute mimesis might be seen as efforts to
copy or embody, and thus control, powerful versions of one's self that are
produced elsewhere. Such performative mimesis has no discourse itself and

resists the social construction of it in terms of external social judgments of eccentricity.

Eccentricity, no longer operating under the illusion that family or class is in charge of its own identity, is an effort to recapture the power or aspects of the self that are constantly being produced elsewhere. The eccentric self is nothing other than this engagement with its dynamic peripheries and has no center itself (i.e., no self-consciousness of a centered self)—such a self is thus literally off-center or ec-centric.

Descriptively, the strength of this argument about the mimetic nature of eccentricity in contexts of great wealth, fame, and power depends on demonstrating in particular cases the relationship of obsessions and fetishes to the hidden worlds of agency in which one is keenly aware that one's self and identity are being authored elsewhere. And the frame for thinking about this is the two arguments about the alternative sources of contemporary dynastic authority with which I began this essay: eccentric mimesis oriented to the world of wealth and public image in the hands of a division of expert labor, and eccentric mimesis oriented to the ancestor, who, through the power of evaluative character discourse that permeates families of dynastic descendants, inhabits the body and mind of the heir.

Regarding eccentric mimesis oriented to agencies of self production in the worlds of wealth, expertise, and public relations that construct dynasty, it is useful to think of the situation as ironically the reverse of Marx's famous commodity fetishism, in which the hidden relations of persons are visibly manifested in the relations of things (through the autonomy of the economy): for dynastic descendants, hidden relations of things (the production of persons as wealth shares, traded, invested, and circulated as abstract economic value) are manifested directly through the visible relations of persons belonging to dynastic families among themselves and toward others. The doppelganger clink of money is the parallel world that constantly inhabits the immediate life world of the dynastic heir.

In his study of the socialization of children of privilege in American society, Robert Coles conjured this through the trope of "entitlement":

> I use the word "entitlement" to describe what, perhaps, all quite well-off American families transmit to their children—an important psychological common denominator, I believe: an emotional expression, really, of those familiar, class-bound prerogatives, money and power. The word was given to me, amid much soul-searching, by the rather rich parents of a child I began to talk with almost two decades ago, in 1959. I have watched those parents become grandparents, seen what they described as "the responsibilities of entitlement" get handed down to a new generation. When the father, a lawyer and stockbroker

from a prominent and quite influential family, referred to the "entitlement" his
children were growing up with, he had in mind a social rather than a psychological phenomenon: the various juries or committees that select the Mardi Gras
participants in New Orleans' annual parade and celebration. He knew that his
daughter was "entitled" to be invited here. . . . He wanted, however, to go
beyond that social fact; he wanted his children to feel obligated by how fortu-
nate they were, and would no doubt always be. . . . He talked about what he
had received from his parents and what he would give to his children, "auto-
matically, without any thought," and what they too would pass on. The father
was careful to distinguish between the social entitlement and "something else,"
a "something else" he couldn't quite define but he knew he had to try to evoke
if he were to be psychologically candid. . . . "My wife didn't know what I was
talking about when I first used the word. She thought it had something to do
with our ancestry! Maybe it does! I don't mean to be snide. I just think our
children grow up taking a lot for granted, and it can be good that they do, and
it can be bad. It's like anything else; it all depends. I mean, you can have spoiled
brats for children, or you can have kids who want to share what they have. I
don't mean give away all their money! I mean be responsible, and try to live up
to their ideals" (1977, 363–364).

Coles's construct from his data here is just one of many rationales for the
situation among the wealthy and heirs to wealth, which evokes the sense
that the wealthy person is distinctive and not ordinary by the responsible
connection she or he has to the lives of others, which in some unspecified way
constitutes the heir's own. There are various sorts of uncritical, self-satisfying
rationales and rationalizations for accepting this condition as a bearer of
wealth and privilege, like the attitude of entitlement that Coles explores
above. But eccentrics, in short, are those heirs who refuse (feel compelled
not?) to accept such rationales. Instead, they try to get beyond the fetishized
(in the Marxist sense) immediate relations that hide the money and power
relations that lay behind them, and deal directly with the constructions of self
that these impersonal spheres produce. The various categories of eccentric
behaviors mentioned in the previous section can be understood as different
sorts of tactics for so doing. But, as suggested, such behaviors as tactics are
not self-conscious, but rather are mimetic—behaviors seeking connection,
embodiment, perhaps power, over one's self produced by the manipulation
of money or image. The eccentric child of wealth, thus, might radically cut
himself off from the immediate everyday privileges of wealth through living
the life of an impoverished hermit while in seclusion trying to manipulate,
acting extravagantly in, the very unseen spheres of wealth in which his self
has its strongest existence and effects. In the space of seclusion, that other
world is manipulated through indices, icons, and representatives from that

unseen world of one's true existence. Such indeed is the eccentricity of How-ard Hughes, as we will explore further in the next section.

Regarding eccentric mimesis oriented to the unseen world of ancestral authority embodied in oneself by the inculcation of character discourse, the focus is upon bodily obsessions. Many persons as they grow older find them-selves uncannily repeating the habits, looks, and peculiarities of particular forebears, but this sensation is generally much more salient in families defined by ideologies of descent and dynastic authority. Eccentricity is the extreme case of this—what I have called the dynastic uncanny. The descendant's self becomes synonymous with the ancestor's through the bodily and behavioral imitation of a dominant forebear. Luigi Pirandello's Moscarda (1990) is a poignant case: a young man of prominent family who looking in the mirror one day notices a feature of his nose that reminds him of his father and trans-forms his existence. He ends by giving away the family property, to the con-sternation of the local gentry. This may appear to be extreme self-awareness, but really it is the extreme awareness of the other—one's double—which mysteriously and irresistibly inhabits one's self that one had thought to be integral, separate, and distinct. In traditional societies the ancestral sphere is separate from and parallel to that of everyday life, but for eccentric descen-dants it invades one's body and behavior, as a form of possession. Again, my suggestion is that certain behaviors characteristic of eccentrics might be understood in terms of mimetic ancestral doubling within a living descendant who has become the ancestor while still being him- or herself. Eccentricity is the expression and management of this mimetic doubling.

THE CASE OF HOWARD HUGHES

Howard Hughes is one of those famous eccentrics—perhaps the most famous in the recent past—the mere telling of whose biography defines the nature of eccentricity. The latter became possible, following his death in 1976, when a spate of very detailed works on Hughes appeared. Perhaps the most detailed biography was by Donald Barlett and James Steele (1979). From the perspec-tive of this chapter, the major limitation of this work is the authors' assump-tion that Hughes's eccentricities were intended or willed dimensions of his personality. For them, Hughes' eccentricities—his closely guarded privacy, his extravagant and reckless investment projects, the personal risks he took as a pilot—were motivated by the desire to preserve the integrity of self, even to make a monument of it. For example, as they conclude, "From the begin-ning, Howard Hughes had an overpowering urge to become a legend in his own lifetime. He wanted the world to notice and to marvel at what it saw. He wanted to show others that he was every bit the man his father had been" (1979, 622)

My alternative, which I believe is as consistent with the evidence, if not more so, is that Hughes had hardly any self-awareness at all. He certainly was not a person who desired to inflate something that was hardly existent as a self-conscious, centered construct. Instead, Hughes controlled vast resources and businesses from hermitlike, ascetic, even mortifying isolation, protected and exquisitely served by Mormon attendants in what amounted to the systematic annihilation of an integral, centered self in the effort to observe, manipulate, and control the representations of his self that were created in the disembodied management of the various projects of his immense inherited fortune.

Hughes was intimately present among all of these projects and wealth constructions through a massive flow of memoranda and directives. After a career as a shy, reticent Hollywood film magnate and aeronautics entrepreneur, Hughes retreated to a suite of rooms at his Desert Inn in Las Vegas from which he ran his empire by memos for most of the rest of his life. One has to picture an unkempt man living in filth, on a starvation diet, most of the time naked, who nonetheless made his presence felt through memos in a number of complex business deals that involved him in CIA operations, land deals, government military contracts, and organized crime interests. Although sometimes his executives, intermediaries, and assistants populating the complex structure of his interests were out of his control, it is remarkable given the primitive and withdrawn personal conditions in which he lived how much rational direction Hughes in fact exercised over his empire. To me, this is consistent with the basic condition of the wealthy dynastic eccentric oblivious to personal conditions but vibrantly operating in terms of his doubled selves, produced by the agents and agencies that manage his wealth.

Barlett and Steele note that even as Hughes's mental condition deteriorated over the years,

> he never forgot that the outside world would not look kindly on his bizarre behavior, and so he took great pains to keep it a secret and to perpetuate the image he had so carefully nurtured. How else can his remarkable performance in the 1972 telephone press conference be explained? The Hughes who spoke to newsmen that day had spent the previous fifteen years in complete seclusion, going nude daily; allowing his hair, fingernails, and toenails to grow for months; refusing to bathe; urinating in jars, sealing the jars, and storing them in his bedroom closet; and living in mortal fear of germs. Yet when newsmen discreetly asked him to comment on wild rumors about his personal habits and appearance, Hughes chuckled and put them at ease. Yes, he too had seen a

sketch of himself in a magazine showing him with hair falling about his shoulders and nails curling over the ends of his fingers. "The first thing I said was how in the hell could I sign documents that I have been signing," he told the reporters. "I would have gotten tangled up in these fingernails . . . I have always kept my fingernails at a reasonable length . . . I take care of them the same way I always have—the same way I did when I went around the world and times when you have seen me and at the time of the flight of the flying boat, and *every other occasion I have come in contact with the press.*" (1979, 626; italics mine)

One of the contexts in which Hughes's disembodied self had always lived was the creations of the image makers of the media, and he did not disappoint them on this occasion. It was Hughes's many eccentric obsessions of separation and withdrawal that kept him an empty center, so that his complete attention was directed to managing his multiple authored doubled selves, not particularly in the interest of making a legend of any essential self—of which he was not aware—but of participating in the many selves and different spheres that his parallel world of hidden wealth created. As Barlett and Steele note, Hughes had a keen sense of affairs and human nature far from himself, but not in direct relations:

> While Hughes's mind was adept at absorbing complicated technical material, there was no place in it for human beings. Yet despite his inability to relate individually either to men or to women, Hughes displayed a surprising grasp of human nature. He knew what motivated people—their hunger for wealth, their thirst for power, their fascination with sex . . . [yet] Hughes's estrangement from other human beings went a long way toward explaining the demeaning way in which he treated so many people [around him], orchestrating their daily lives down to and including instructions on what food they should eat and where they should park their cars. (1979, 623–624)

Thus, he lived fully at a distance in the abstract worlds of wealth and power in which his doubled self was decisive and vital, and hardly at all in his immediate day-to-day world of controlling obsessions.

ECCENTRICITY ON THE EDGES

In my own experience with dynasties, I met no Howard Hughes nor any family in which the strain of eccentricity had become its collective preoccupation, an ideology of distinction of the last resort, as among, for example, Boston aristocrats of the nineteenth century. Still there was what might be identified as eccentric behavior, as developed in this chapter, and a family awareness of it in every family of dynastic descendants with which I became acquainted. For example, the man who made a fetish of work discipline, going ceremoniously to and from his cellar office each day, even though it was never clear what work he actually did there; the woman, a noted collector of antique porcelain, who dressed only in clothes of the 1950s (when she was a teenager), acquired from secondhand shops; the couple who threw lavish parties, in the middle of which they retired for bed; and so on. While each of these instances would need to be studied within its dynastic context (i.e., the context of the doubling of the self by "hidden world" agencies elsewhere), for me, they recall in a parallel way (but of course, situated very differently) the "lads," nonconformist English working-class schoolboys, whom Paul Willis wrote about (1977), and who saw through their immediate relations to the secret, abstract (hidden world?) labor basis of capital.

Likewise, dynastic eccentrics are evoking their abstract doppelganger selves produced as wealth shares and images (rather than labor) in the parallel worlds of wealth, fame, and power, which both serve and dominate dynastic persons. However, while the nonconformity of the working-class lads channels them to the factory floor, dynastic eccentrics are destined for treatment in the world of mental health professionals, or they are left to stagnate in the purgatory of their particular, indulged obsessions. They are then, perhaps, to be finally claimed by their families in decline—losing ground to the dynastic authority of experts and managers—as a replacement for character discourse in a last-ditch grabbing at the residue of family distinction.

REFERENCES

Barlett, Donald L., and James B. Steele. 1979. *The Life, Legend, and Madness of Howard Hughes.* New York: Norton.

Coles, Robert. 1977. *Children of Crisis.* Vol. 5. *Privileged Ones.* Boston: Atlantic-Little, Brown.

Hall, Peter D. 1982. *The Organization of American Culture, 1700–1900: Private Institutions, Elites, and the Origins of American Nationality.* New York: New York University Press.

Marcus, George E., with Peter D. Hall. 1992. *Lives in Trust: The Fortunes of Dynastic Families in Late Twentieth Century America.* Boulder: Westview Press.

Pirandello, Luigi. 1990. *One, No One, and One Hundred Thousand.* Translated by William Weaver. Boston: Eridanos Press.

Sass, Louis A. 1992. *Madness and Modernism: Insanity in the Light of Modern Art, Literature, and Thought.* New York: Basic Books.

Taussig, Michael. 1992a. *Mimesis and Alterity.* New York: Routledge.

———. 1992b. "Physiognomic Aspects of Visual Worlds." *Visual Anthropology Review* 8:15–28.

Weeks, David Joseph, with Kate Ward. 1988. *Eccentrics: The Scientific Investigation.* London: Stirling University Press.

Willis, Paul. 1977. *Learning to Labour.* New York: Columbia University Press.

FOUR

If You Have the Advertisement You Don't Need the Product

Roy Wagner

One of the lessons of the Cold War era has to do with families of American military personnel living at bases in Germany, the Philippines, and elsewhere. Often these people would ask friends and relatives back in the States to send them videotapes of American television programming. Their requests made it clear, however, that although footage of sporting events, sitcoms, and soap operas was welcome, what they really wanted was commercial footage—advertising. Though they had the products, or could easily get them at the military store, and could view other peoples' ads, often of the same products, in other languages, they wanted something else, wanted the ads, in American.

So the lesson is one of style or lifestyle, which has to do with the featuring of products or logos more than the products themselves, with the ways in which people are featured in products and products featured in people. Where the consumer world is bigger, more potent, than the things consumed, so that consumption becomes its own message, wanting is more important than needing. One might say that the expatriate families wanted the "America" that video ads often apostrophize, something that the slang of the twenties called a "bromide," and wanted it more than the Americans who happen to live there.

The lesson of an America made contingent in its wants rather than its needs, that wants to be featured for itself more than it wants social programs, health care benefits, or something called "family values," is a lesson about a wholly contingent family. That bromide, as it were, is only contingent to the one that David Schneider describes in *American Kinship* (1968), is not related by ties of substance or code for conduct, and is fundamentally embarrassed by them. It tries, nonetheless, very hard in the half-life it lives between commercial breaks, in sitcoms, in soap opera scenarios, and sometimes in the

59

ads themselves, to rediscover the moral, the substance, and the code, and make them its own. Very often political candidates or TV evangelists step in to lend it a helping hand.

What I am talking about is the advertising image and its associated programming as the primary mode of consumption in America—the wanting that steals the show from using, or even liking. It has nothing whatever to do with the question of whether advertising "works" in the sense of persuading people to buy products or ogle logos, and is oblivious to the fact that important sectors of the economy do minimal advertising, or none at all. Like the stock exchange or the futures market, it is only a focus placed within the larger focus of the economy, prodigious only in its ability to subvert.

I shall deal with the consuming image in terms of a performative mode that I propose to call the self-act. I shall argue that a particular mode of self-enactment, cognitively opaque and almost autistic in behavioral terms, is a diagnostic or diacritical feature of much commercial and noncommercial video programming. The self-act is a contagious image of consumption, something that can easily be seen to imitate almost anything else, and depends upon one's own reaction to it, and thus one's own self-action, for its interpretive scope. It does not, otherwise, interpret the self, is not "about" the self that it performs, has no self-awareness in it, and is less a postmodern message than it is a postmodern decoy. As a masterstroke of video typecasting it leaves narcissism far behind. In relative terms it captures the essence of pop music performance; in absolute terms it is a semiotic joke.

The really spontaneous self-action that might be identified with choice or volition is not something that is visible save in its effects. There is simply no way of knowing whether "spontaneity" itself would have anything to do with its effects or circumstances, or with the chains of necessity that we associate with causality or significance. Yet without its staging or representation in one way or another, the America of code and conduct, of money and value, would fall apart into its unmediated primitives. It is crucial to a comprehension of its flexibility in this to realize that the self-act is not an act of "building" nor a "built" or constructed thing. It is not a social dance or a "text" with implicit messages worked into it and not an inherently "meaningful" performance at all. Because it is "about" product consumption in a subjective sense, as the subject of consumption, advertisement need not be about the product or logo, which it involves contingently, nor about the equally contingent consumer. People are about *it* in somewhat the same way as the product is about it, and it is the contingency of each to the other that the ad performs or replaces.

Since products are not actors save in contingencies of this sort, or more directly since the ad world is contrived so as to feature them that way, the human coefficient of this performative bears some examining. The graphic instance of human beings engaged in the intimate performance of one another's self-action is erotic, though not necessarily sexual. For purposes of video presentation it is eminently divisible into a variety of forms of self-action that in some way indicate an other: autoerotic, self-questioning, self-blaming, accident-prone, and so forth. The TV family of the 1980s is a group of generally disparate people related to each other by their own peculiar varieties of self-action. Whether they occur in sitcoms, cartoons, or as guest-adulterers on talk shows, they are there for a particular reason. The reason is not sociological and it is not generic—because television had Archie and Edith, the Jeffersons, or the Brady Bunch. Their presence is necessary to fulfill the myth of the autoreactive product/person, turn it into the kind of relational daisy chain that we like to feature as a necessary backdrop for American life.

There is then a question, closely related to that of manipulation in advertising and other media presentations, of whether the contingent America is in fact a cultural construction. If "construction" implies a kind of artifactual representation, contriving for oneself or for others the stuff, perhaps symbolic, of which meaningful interpretations are made, then the question comes down to that of who makes the image, or images the making. The America that wants, gimme America, is really a sort of negative image, as Hegel, for instance, spoke of hunger, or desire, or hope as particular forms of emptiness that exist by virtue of wanting to be filled with something (Kojève 1980). It is not, so to speak, your father's Oldsmobile, not the America that has blood kinship, already reproduced relatives, God bless them, or codes for appropriate and inappropriate conduct. These are already filled with something. Unconstructed, perhaps unreconstructed, contingent America exists as a construction for those who have a certain theory about how construction takes place, or would like to have one, in the way that literary criticism learns how to unpack a text by working assiduously at packing it.

That sort of thing is admissible in the interpretive sciences; more than that, it is expected. But in advertising it would give the game away, would be your father's Oldsmobile. Actually constructing the desire for a product, shaping the America that wants upon the last of one's logo would close self-consumption out of its own picture. What it does to you is what you do to yourself, and the way it does this is by being about itself. So the contingent American, the advertising consumer, if that being has a separable existence, may or may not have a coherent idea of what the advertiser has in mind, but whether the consumer has such an idea or not is as immaterial to the advertising as automobile styling is to a contemporary aesthetic. The shaping of car bodies is as much an art of self-parody as any other aspect of advertising; it does not have to conform to an aesthetic because it is only imitating its own version of one. Cars that range from the marginally acceptable to the downright hideous, domestic imitations of imports and vice versa, do not so much adapt to a common taste as they adapt that taste, and it is a taste wherein wanting is more important than liking.

As against the local, or regional, and largely newspaper advertising that makes the product and its qualities incidental to a statement about *availability* ("no money down," "Easy Jack's Appliances," "twenty stores near you"), sophisticated ads make the product incidental to something else. It is rather important that the "something else," apostrophized as "you" or "America," and perhaps glossable as a "self," has no real existence as such. What I have termed "gimme America" is not encountered outside of its advertisements, sitcoms, and the like; it imitates a life, like that of the movies, that is never lived, and must for that reason imitate it very closely. The virtual reality of an "almost life" is on its terms more real than that which it imitates. Like the fractal imaging of virtual reality programs, and like a constructionalist emplotment of "cultural meaning," it keeps the same degree of detail no matter how great the magnification.

Public service or "outreach" ads—"stay in school," "don't mess with drugs," "say no to family abuse"—are no less part of the "something else," no matter how laudable their motives, that products incidentalize themselves to. By the time you have figured out that the pitch is not the "telephone Granny sometimes" of the big communications nets, your motive in trying to figure it out is supposed to have become something social, a kind of unpersuasion of gimme America that is nonetheless addressed to gimme America. It is not unlikely that social messages disguised as advertising and advertising disguised as social message have roughly the same effect, having the same audience. Would that effect, and that audience, be any different if drugs were legalized as lotteries have been, or beer or automobiles certified, like tobacco, as health hazards?

There is also the advertising of news coverage, "we are always there, night or day, rain or shine, and especially disasters." If advertising is supposed to be news, then news itself can be advertised; if coverage is a product, then news is the example par excellence of product availability, the discourse that marks itself off as the availability of event. But with this particular product, "coverage," you don't have to buy anything at all—someone else pays for it, and pays a lot. Here, as in outreach ads, it is your motive in watching it that is bought and sold, as well as acted out, by somebody else. In a rather McLuhanesque fashion, the disaster is its own disaster, gets to be more and more that way as coverage increases and commentators expand upon it, and becomes the enactment of its own newsworthiness.

Coverage is then perhaps the ongoing promise of construction; it will be there when it is needed. But the disaster itself belongs to the family of causes, like the product, the political or social cause, or the family itself, that represents the need for a need. Need exponential is something superimposed upon one's needs and upon the rhetoric of need; it exposes or represents the needy through the solicitation of need, imitates wanting in the realm of necessities. It is the stuff of which charities are made, as well as political campaigns and of course millenarian movements. When it is satisfied one needs more, and those who have become dependent on this mode of self-consumption are likely to suffer its absence as a kind of letdown, an empty space where the need for needing belongs.

Thus the whole power of construction, if that is the word, in this medium is shifted from an arbitrary empty space of responsible necessity to a much more intimate and proximal one called "wanting." Once this shift has been accomplished, needs and their construction will take care of themselves, and their rhetoric merely serves to underscore the fact. It is because need is only imitated in performing the need for it that advertising and social or political messaging come off as excusable, like an incidental conversation with oneself carried on by others. What it masks most in its performance of intimated desires and desired intimacies, of TV families and family-oriented TV, is the ultimate dependency of its self- and other-imitating resources upon the phenomenon of "scope."

This is at once technological and social, and it is marked by the penetration of multifocal and "scoping" devices, not all of them electronic, into all aspects and classes of modern life. The instant inventory or schematic display, the coverage of coverage that tells who is watching the watching of the world and so helps to persuade the persuaders, the needs of assessment that dictate the needs of education, are diagnostic examples. If the image itself is regarded as insidious, an imitator of intentionality, we must not forget its imitative counterpart in the intended.

What has happened is that the perceptual technology of written representation, with its contingent conceptions of the sign and the possibility of constructing an analytic language about language, has been upstaged by a perceptualist self-act, a scoping of the scope. A scholarship of "constructionism" is reduced to finding segmental or semiotic equivalents, analytic "redescriptions," for images that do not need them, trading on the marginal advantage through which its anthropology has exploited so-called oral literatures and indigenous poetics. It gives us what we need to convince ourselves that there is, if not a deep structure or core symbolism at work in the "culturing" of things, at least an ongoing work of assemblage in their lived experience. A scopic prose makes all of this unnecessary, not by resuscitating oral tradition and turning the world, as Marshall McLuhan has suggested, into a global village, but by imitating insight in its own artifact, making its own presentation the need for a need, as advertising does. A succession of images with or without verbal continuity does much the same thing; as video footage or cinematics it represents its own continuity as if human experience and the "self" it indexes were lived and known intimately as a narrative sequence, a kind of "psycho-footage."

It simply does not matter at this point whether the self and its self-experiencing is *really* constituted temporal-ly or in a sequential or quasi-narrative fashion. How could we really know? Scopism, like advertising, makes its own virtue out of our inability to know this by imitating the experience of knowing within the self-mapping of experience. Never mind the biases of the commentator or the subtle innuendos in advertising that may be erotic and can always be demonstrated as such by inventing a subconscious for them. Critiques that take as their main point the necessary or intentional superadding of bias and "hidden persuaders" are merely entering into the consumer's prerogative in a novel and critical way, recreating "need" as bias from the need for a need already performed. It is not as if advertisers, who are often their own best persuaders, do not sometimes do this themselves, or commentators from time to time make the news their own, but that an added "spin" of this sort is incidental to the capturing of its needs through self-action. Often enough advertisers are avid copiers of the critiques made of their art, and one would like to imagine them constructing themselves as Evil Persons. Perhaps for this very reason, their self-consciousness as manipulators, they might be the first to cry "unfair advantage" if a cigarette manufacturer marketed a product called "Coffin Nails" or "SURGEON GENERAL'S WARNING," trading on the macho of death rather than that of cowboys or tattoos.

A certain degree of conscious manipulation, or at least the illusion of it, is as necessary in advertising as it is in government or high finance, if only to assure the agents that they are in control, or that control is possible. Though conscious manipulation, for what it's worth, can easily be turned around into the manipulation of consciousness, the piloting of public awareness, it raises the question of whether or not the self is to be equated with consciousness—the "conscious self" that carries so much weight in phenomenological literature or postmodern writing. Yet if consciousness is defined in this way as the self, the being one is, it is not unlikely that one will come up with something that "works" incidentally to the main action, like the self-persuaded manipulator of advertising. What if the self were rather something like the autonomic nervous system or the autoimmune system, agencies (whatever agencies may be) that are less subconscious than they are nonconscious, much better at acting as if they were aware than at really being aware?

The fact is that when anything of this sort is suspected of being more aware of us than we are—a brain or some other aspect of the nervous system, a subconscious, a transcendental ego, or a luminous energy aura imagined as the agency of spontaneity—then it is the way that agency becomes perceptible and tractable that steals the show. That is the essence of what I have called "scopism." The subconscious is a creation of the rhetorical metaphors of "unpacking" it, the imaged brain or electronically magnified neuronic activity is the subject of a clinical video program with no commercials. The secret of the scope is that it can never and need never reach closure, show the shape and form of the self-act and the need for a need that it projects; it can only redescribe one aspect of common experience in terms of another. Fundamentally retrogressive and recapitulative, it shows you what you are all about or what it is all about, turns history into anatomy and anatomy into history.

What is going on here is very simple and is directly pertinent to the kinds of cultural problems that advertising brings to the fore. Neither the self nor the special attributes of consciousness or spontaneity that advertising implicates itself within are necessary to human life or even to thinking about human life and its conditions. It is rather that advertising and the media, as well as the phenomenon of "scope" that is instantiated through them, have the effect of making human life and its familiar conditions necessary to their own conception. This means that "self" and the reflexivity implied in the term is like a ventriloquist effect or an illusion of depth within the familiar. Examples of this déjà vu and its petitioned necessities are not hard to find in natural science speculation, like the "selfish gene" that makes the power and passion of phenotypic existence necessary to its reproductive ends, or the so-called anthropic principle by which the universe evolved human beings so as to see and know itself. The difference in advertising is that it foregrounds causality in the concrete and familiar rather than the abstract.

So perhaps the Americans at foreign military bases who requested commercial footage wanted only a performative quitclaim on the self, wanted to witness their need for a need properly taken care of. It is difficult to tell because it is *always* difficult to say anything at all about the putative construction of a self. The subjective is never properly "subjective" until it has been in some way objectified, the pain referred, the dream narrated again if only in one's head. At that point one is dealing with a description on behalf of the described, the "performance" of that which has been made necessary to something else. What I have called the "need for a need" simply describes this contingency of the subjective, as what we may call the "performative" aspect of the media performs it. But the performance of a need for a need is just as much a way out of the self as it may be a way into it.

So the proverbial observer from Mars, or nowadays from Alpha Centauri or the Pleiades, might conclude that there is an elaborate dance or mime that Americans know as the product. And that naive observer might also note that the jazzing of the soft drink, buffooning of the pizza, or body-pantomime of a motorcar never takes place in real life. There is no question of "materialism" here, nor do these disingenuous constructions even imply it. The social, "America" and its family, is not materialistic in this message so much as the material is inherently social, demonstrative, extraverted. What this has to say about the "America" cheated of its very materialism, the cold-eyed terrestrial that, according to candid polls, is likely to keep a loaded firearm in its automobile and hold its opinions very close to its chest, is a very intriguing question.

A functional model, the stock-in-trade of flowcharts, engineering diagrams, and economic or social planning, will always find its object in some sense wanting, for supply and demand, or cause and effect, is how that object has been constructed. But a structural model, one that shows "construction" itself as the object of function, takes the description as the basis of need and is vulnerable only in the static character of the formalism that it puts in place of function. The only way out of the formal dilemma is to consider how the structure may be self-performed or self-enacted within the issues or circumstances of its description. That is what is meant by the "construction" of a text, or of a self, a product, or a person. And if it is the issue that is taken up, or discerned and brought into focus, that makes the difference between static formalism and what Marshall Sahlins would call the "structure of the conjuncture" (1985, esp. vii ff.), then that is why contemporary anthropology has become an "issue-ology." It is why culture, the formal system, has been abandoned for the ethnicity that performs the cultural in search of its authenticity, and why the study of gender is primarily concerned with the social, political, or activist causes within which gender is featured rather than with some model of what gender may be.

The self-performative enactment or issue does not, on this understanding, respond to a need; it is not functional, nor does it describe itself save in terms of its own exigency. It throws its own functional or structural implications into diacritical relief, into "scare" quotes. Once the self-performative enactment has been "discovered" in this way, it becomes very difficult to persuade oneself that all social or cultural phenomena do not enact themselves in the same format, and so the whole of social science theory is thrown into scare quotes. If such a discovery amounts to what is called a "postmodern" or "poststructural" crisis, and thus inadvertantly puts itself into scare quotes, that is because it advertises itself in the same way that the advertised product discovers itself, by imagining self-performance as the performance of a "self."

Performing the necessity of one's own issue is an act of invention, literally of enfolding oneself within the issue. It has the subjective valence or "feel" of discovering something about others in one's own action, or what is called consciousness raising. And it has the objective valence of turning the imitation of self into something that looks and feels like conviction, of a moment of truth so full of the truth of the moment that the participant has to be reminded of the name or the logo of the sponsor. One important consequence of self-making is that the principles and legitimacy of the act are made derivative or epiphenomenal to the act itself; they become, in the scare quotes of everyday parlance, "causes."

This is what advertising, or the "self" and its dubious phenomenology, peddles—not the product or the cultural and psychological legitimacy, but the effect that will make the cause necessary to its own enactment. It is in its way the opposite of shamanic curing. The shaman's vision is completely autoscopic; nobody sees it but the shaman, to whom it makes the other world visible. But video imaging turns the tables; it is heteroscopic and makes negotiable an objectified world of the self. The shaman in Lévi-Strauss's famous essay "The Sorcerer and His Magic" (1963) does not cheat because the objects sucked or produced from the patient's body are in any case surrogates, intentional fakes, for the curative extraction of subliminal causes. Video imaging never cheats either; it brings one to marvel at the transformations finessed through known techniques of image programming, an obvious and performed mimicry rather than a secretly mimicked performance. It does not extract subliminal causes but introjects obvious ones—the news events, products, and problem scenarios that foreground need's need.

The authority for the shaman's vision is private; it is privileged by beings and powers that live the half-life of publicly performed cures and accounts, proxies for the person who objectifies them. Heteroscopic powers, the "news-face" of the commentator or public figure, the quality-face of the product, the logo, or the advocacy-construct live a different sort of half-life, no less public, that we call "image." The image is no more a self than is the shaman's spirit-helper; the difference lies in the fact that it is manifested subjectively rather than objectively, a quality of mind, an *emotion* that is spread abroad. In this sense the image belongs neither to the viewer nor the telecaster; it has the autonomy of the shaman's spirit-powers without privileging anybody's vision. And so it turns the tables on responsibility and is not a proxy for the viewer who stands in front of it or the sponsor who stands behind it.

In apposite contrast to the claimed vision of the shaman, contested at the peril of supernatural retribution, the image is a contested vision claimed at the peril of public responsibility. It is not that the viewer, the subject of "try it, you'll like it," or the producer or public figure is its proxy. It is rather that each "side" of the image is trying valiantly with polls, investigations, and sometimes accusations, to get the other to stand proxy for it. A shaman's view of his or her own profession is that of having been put on the spot: "dammit I would have died otherwise, and as a matter of fact I did." But putting someone else on the spot comes down to the same thing: "I did it for the sake of image," or "image made me do it."

Like the unowned image, only part of which is under anyone's direct influence, heteroscopy is entirely transparent. Others can see it and know it, but an important aspect of the transparency implies the seeing and knowing of others as well, and the focality of the concept exploits the highly ambiguous relativity of these two potentials.

What is a "heteroscope"? It is important not to confuse the idea and its quasi-cultural, quasi-psychological, quasi-literary insinuations with the technology that facilitated it. Cybernetics and television were the "hot news" of the 1940s and early 1950s, the era of the "atom bomb," of the wizard-physicist, of Howdy Doody, Captain Video, and Super Circus. This was a time when video, or nukes, or computers could be their own messages as the relatively undeveloped technology they were. It was necessary for the "programming" that we associate in two different senses with video and computers, and for technology itself, to become not only sophisticated but also thoroughly familiar for the heteroscope to solidify itself. As language is for the native speaker, or as *hands,* for instance, are for the neurophilosopher, it was imperative that the means of the heteroscope become too close to the field of action to be noticed. An "artificial intelligence," or a technology that may imitate the mind or its products, is the product we see, one side of heteroscopy. But it is not heteroscopic in the full sense—it does not deserve the "post" before its modernity—until we get the other side, the self or person, call it what you will, that imitates the technology of doing so.

The *objectivity* of telecasting, "letting you see what we see" by virtue of "letting us see what you see," is intimately related to the motivation of another fundamentally popular device that might be called the "socioscope." Telecasting is objective about its coverage, and coverage is objective about the view that is taken. In a like manner the sociology of polls, statistics, and surveys is something of a misnomer even in its own objectivist terms. It does not measure "society," whatever that might be, but something entirely different; it measures the *scope* of society, the degree of its relative transparency to itself. As Stephen Jay Gould tells us in *The Mismeasure of Man* (1981), most of the refinements of statistics have come about through the attempt to measure human intelligence, that is, to force closure on the human ability to comprehend what human beings are about. Socioscopic prose can afford to be entirely objective because its object is itself.

Exaggerated to the parameters of a concept, this identification of the known with the ability to know becomes anthroscopic, the model of the "culture" as the model you can make of it. For all that "others," indigenous folk and so forth, must do the same thing, it is not the objectivity of the model that is problematic but the rhetoric necessary to make it "fit" with an arbitrarily conceived notion of the social or the collective, to assert the "scope" as a collectively held potential. This fact does not demolish the culture-concept at all, but obviates instead its "telecasting," the spurious sociology that is read into it. In straightforward terms it reaffirms culture as something essentially exotic to those who identify with it, study it, or attempt to describe it. Culture stands in relation to the attempts made to own it or understand it as a joke does to the humor that is made of it; we laugh at ourselves instead, with the joke as the need for our need to do so.

The interpretive sciences do not have a very convincing arsenal of concepts to deal with folks who do not care very much about what they are doing, or who only pretend to care. Theories about people caught in their own webs of meaning, or culture internalized, or about reality-scenarios plotted out subliminally in the head, are historical ones dating from the days of the scientific test designed to prove which cleanser cleans best, or before. It is the scope of the media performance, and the ideology necessary to the self-transparency of the scope, that is "performative," and the specific act, or scenario, or symbol, is only contingently performed within the assumptions of that ideology.

An ad, or a sitcom or interview, that merely juxtaposes the components or images of what might be used to construct meaningfulness has no necessarily psychological or symbolic content in and of itself. To say that it interprets the audience or that the audience interprets it is to add an entirely correlative sense of agency, an ad hoc theory of psychologism or sign-instrumentality to a circumstance that can function very well without interpretation of any sort. If the same ambivalent juxtaposition of contingent imageries were videotaped as a "ritual," say in an Amazonian village, with feathers and body paint for special effects, one might easily be led to believe it was a profound interpretive statement by the people about their world. Possibly local informants might even be found to interpret it in that way. One might ask, however, once the indigenous and exogenous interpreters have done their jobs, just exactly *whose* scope, whose care or concern, whose "self" or meanings we are talking about.

No self-respecting colonialist regime of the late nineteenth century would have permitted the extent of starvation, malnutrition, and refugeeism, the leveling of rain forests and human resources, that are a normal part of our world. Heads would have rolled, and they would not have been malnourished ones. If we seem to need those self-important patronizers of the third world now more than ever for the readjustment of our own attitudes, is it not because the sense of agency that they once turned into imperial aggrandizement has been gifted to the scope itself, to the sign and symbol and the interpretive power of revisiting one's own perspectives?

"Multiculture" is the same substitution of image for effectiveness on a global or pan-ethnic scale as contingent "America" and the TV family are on that of the scope as product. Caring is turned into seeing and seeing is turned into caring. Foregrounding needs and concerns that are largely extraneous to that which is represented, and that belong to the contingencies of representation itself, models of and models for the activity of modeling, scopism skims the cream off a largely indifferent world, recreates care and concern in its own rhetorical image. All of the objective and instrumentive features that we associate with the sign or symbol—indexic and iconic qualities, liminality, the pragmatic purchase over the human subject and its reactions—are contained within the musculature and quizzical mechanism of that rhetoric.

If we consider such disparate historical phenomena as Shakespeare's Globe theater, Galileo's telescope, visual art including the camera, and the space program not as human discoveries but as specific discoveries of the human, then television and computers are not accidental breakthroughs. Like the strange and evasive notion of "culture" and the equally evasive idea of the "self" and its consciousness, they instantiate a power of image over the imaged, and over the imagers. All of these share a kind of falsification, which may be admired or disparaged, and is commonly both admired and disparaged: that of the human control of iconic deception, the *trompe l'oeil* ("fooling the eye") of Baroque painting, or the technological and semiotic efforts to define the image. Behind the deception involved in imitating human perception and reaction better than they can imitate themselves lies the coordinate moral dilemma of the discovery of the human, or what could be called the problem of the "double." What the falsification falsifies is the image that wants to be human, the Pinocchiolike personification of the product, the personae of the androids in Isaac Asimov's robot novels, the ambition of Mr. Data in the *Star Trek: The Next Generation* series.

What advertising's product, or logo, "does for you" and what the computer or sociometric "society" images for you is always a version of that being's asymptotic imitation of the human. The problem, which might have haunted Pinocchio's varnished nightmares quite as much as Data's positronic ones, is that for them success would mean failure. It is the *difference* between their imitations and the humanity they imitate that makes them valuable, that makes "society" or "the economy" measurable and thinkable as an excrescence in its own right, and makes "consciousness," or "morality," or "culture," something that human beings can imagine themselves to be doing. It is the *difference* that makes them human and not the human that makes the difference.

As immortals who find the concept of death very intriguing, homunculi play the role of "the gods" in Heraclitus's cryptic observation "they live our deaths as we live theirs"; their needs are the need for ours. The *personhood* that surfaces under the most wildly improbable circumstances—fossil humans and extraterrestrials, fiction characters and personal divinities no less than TV families, doughboys, and rubbery pizza-people—is not motivated by sign-functions, economic necessities, or lifestyles, but rather motivates them. It makes the difference of the product, the past or future, the soul, the ethnicity, the American Way of Life. When the economy breaks down or semioticists come to doubt the autonomy of the sign, we tend to set up elaborate receiving gear to intercept its messages from far out in the galaxy. What if we got an SOS: "Never mind your products, your docudramas and silly serials; send us your needs, send us a starship called Enterprise"?

Personhood, the self, is just that critical side of the subject matter that meaning and agency, the definitional apparatus of an instrumentive inquiry, cannot reach, and for the simple reason that it is trying to reach us. In whatever form the scope may be rediscovered, its concurrent rediscovery of the human makes other things, other issues, more immediately relevant to the subject than the subject itself, reinvents the image that wants to be human in yet another guise. It is possible to imagine a magical moment in the evolution of any discourse, collective or personal, when the sheer weight of its history forces itself into endless retelling. There are whole civilizations that make maps only of themselves.

As science fiction often enough projects a future "bad life" in its realistic dystopias, anthropology is often accused of seeking a good life, or at least a moral one, in other times and places, or at least of dislocating the life that it finds in the past, as Fabian has suggested (1983). Though advertising mimics science fiction as regularly as it does ethnicity and seems to be more about the good life than anything else, it does not really "do" the future and past in those ways: it regurgitates its slogans and anticipates its consumers to a different end. That end is the "now" or the moment, a non-time that is not simply more difficult to focus than past or future, but in fact is impossible. And if anthropologists as well as science fiction writers have learned that good and bad, moral and immoral, are such contingently relative terms that it is context or quality that matters most in delineating them, advertising deals with context and quality alone. It does not project but introjects, or contextualizes quality, and not necessarily quality of life or product quality, though these may be implied, but just plain quality.

Anthropology might have something to teach the world of advertising, might convince it that it is "selfing" the other or othering the self, colonizing the mind with the product or the product with the mind, that it is maybe a culture in its own right. But advertising, with its fabulous and ephemeral "now" has something to unteach anthropology as well. Are not "self" and "consciousness" simply fancy words, with an inbuilt existential persuasion, for that "now," that all-important moment that is over and done with by the time you think about it? Does not the anthropology that is in love with contemporaneity treat these terms, mostly looted from phenomenology or object-psychology and social critique, as advertising slogans for a product that somehow just misses the quality it is after? For advertising, at least, the product does not matter so much; it is the quality that counts.

For the psychoanalyst, and doubtless the patient in therapy, there is always the possibility of getting *below* the conscious, underwhelming it or at least playing an elaborate game of Dungeons and Dragons in its basement. But the advertising that wants to overwhelm it does not even have a word for the "superconscious" in its most cynical shoptalk, has other words to worry about, and will let go of them in a cold minute if it has to. In that regard the social scientist and the social science subject, the ape that has been taught sign language and lives in the world of the sign, are just poor losers, who hang on to their words for the precious chance to name the thing that is hanging on to them.

There is indeed a lesson here about the sanity or utility of inventing psychological, sociological, or even semiotic theories about representation or objectification and how they may "work." Whatever ad people may think or say among themselves about the imaged "object" dancing, singing, acting crazy, moving deliriously on the screen with no visible means of support, the simplistic spontaneity of the image itself is sufficient to all of it and to much more besides. Does such a proxy for the product "self-image" itself in the memory, so that the slogan or perhaps the product will literally "jump out" at a potential buyer in some later consumer context? ("It is only people having *fun*, great, outrageous, extraordinary fun, a beer commercial for people that actually *fizz*.") Or is it simply that a proxy so energized works primarily because the "memory" that is imagined for it works in precisely the same way?

There is really no need to second-guess an ad of this sort; the need that takes care of any imaginable need to do so is requited in the simple Paul Joseph Goebbels action of repeating it over and over again. An ad just "runs," and any imagined action of persuasion runs along with it. The beer-proxy "drinks" its consumers, regardless of whether or not they are potential customers, the automobile proxy "motivates" believers and unbelievers alike.

It is when the viewer turns off the senses in the delirium tremens of "commercial time" that the "senses" turn the viewer on. Just "trash," news about the product that has become news to itself, it gets on your *nerves*, regardless of what nerves may be or how they may work. It is easy enough to imagine that the rules and conventions of culture have their effect in just the same way, display their moral or normative "printout" precisely because they are so *aggravating*. Rules, as George Papashvili once observed, "are for when the brains give out." It simply does not matter what one *thinks* about them, or even if they are renegotiated—there will always be rules there, things to get on your nerves in that magical moment when the brains have had their say.

That, in its cranial nutshell, is the *scope* or video-image of the moral collectivity that Durkheim wrote about, of the living-room family that sees itself on the screen and the screen family that sees itself in the living room. So pretending that the TV family is a ritual staged carefully between (but also within) commercial breaks is hardly inappropriate even to a Durkheimian sense of ritual. *Any* ritual and any liturgy works that way, too, wrings the rhetorical stuffings out of its audiences and performers.

The anthropology of reflexivity, of the making and breaking of "self," finds its precedence in writers like Benedict and Sapir, as well as in phenomenological pioneers like Husserl, Cassirer, and Merleau-Ponty. It becomes anthropologically viable, something more than psychology or philosophy, when as in the cultural criticism of Foucault, Derrida, and Bourdieu, among others, it draws upon the idea of the social or cultural as a focal catalyst. So it becomes anthropological at the point where anthropology itself becomes reflexive, in a catalysis that becomes "an experience, almost a personal revelation," in the words of Louis Dumont (1970, 5), "and that is why I speak of 'sociological apperception.' " The central tenet of a symbolic or perhaps a structuralist anthropology, that, whatever else it might involve, society becomes "cultural" when its conception of itself is germinal to one's conception of it, lends its emphatic rhetoric to "mind" in just the way that mind furnishes the rhetorical language for the social.

In what way is this fantastic double play of mind and its audience any different from the "sociology" that TV executives might pretend for shows that are substandard imitations of *All in the Family?* If you have the rhetoric of the advertisement, you don't even need the advertisement. If personal idiosyncrasy, that dancing TV object with no visible means of support, provides the rhetoric for society's brainless rules and even the rules' ethical flavor, what is to prevent that utterly insipid ethos from motivating it in the same way? What I have called the TV family has not *replaced* the American family any more than the consuming of food replaces food value. The need for its needs is not something that family or family values could ever address, is necessary in and of itself in a fundamentally different way than the family might be.

There have been no widely held or universally acknowledged theoretical departures in anthropology since the structuralism of Claude Lévi-Strauss and Louis Dumont, no theories proposed that, whatever their merits, have not borrowed their rhetorical motivations from other domains or earlier writers with the single aim of somehow getting beyond structuralism. Such efforts are not poststructuralist or postmodern in any sense, but prestructuralist reversions, attempts at getting back to the kind of focus that structure provided for thought and thought attempted for structure. Because structure is impacted within the very efforts at overcoming its precedence in this way, no one has even suggested *how* the construction of a self, a memory or *the* memory, or a cultural scenario, actually takes place. Apart from various "performative" notions (e.g., an act of constructing that coincides with the motivation for doing it as a sui generis phenomenon), a sort of divination for personal motive, self-interest, social inequality, or exploitation, and other sitcom favorites, provides the rationale.

Perhaps what is most troubling about the rhetorics, popular and academic, that make the self conceivable, and the idea of "self" that makes such reflective structures inevitable, is that the main point seems somehow to have been left out. Whether entertained as a theory or theorized as a mode of entertainment, that point is too precariously situated between the serious and the funny to make any sort of dialectic between the two manageable. The point is not theoretical at all, and still less is it entertaining; it is a lesson about the acute vulnerability of solipsism. What I have called "the need for a need" is personalized in the self-conception of someone who wants to believe that he or she has invented the world whole in the imagination, and so needs the affirmation and the language of others more desperately than those others need him or her.

It is the solipsism inherent in virtually every version of culture theory, however it may be masked as psychology or phenomenology, that brings one to suspect a "politics" behind a theory that has become untenable. But it is also the need for one's need to do so, the rhetorical foil without which politics would be unpersuasive, that brings one to suspect a theory behind the politics one has learned to distrust. Like the married couple that discovered that a self-definition of each as superior to the other forges a bond stronger than love,[1] culturology has discovered how to make the most of its subjectivity. Perhaps that is why those who have tried to teach sign language to apes get mostly obscene messages in return.

NOTES

1. I thank Nancy Zacharius for this illustration.

REFERENCES

Dumont, Louis. 1970. *Homo Hierarchicus.* Translated by M. Sainsbury. Chicago: University of Chicago Press.

Fabian, Johannes. 1983. *Time and the Other: How Anthropology Makes Its Object.* New York: Columbia University Press.

Gould, Stephen Jay. 1981. *The Mismeasure of Man.* New York: Norton.

Kojève, Alexandre. 1980. *Introduction to the Reading of Hegel: Lectures in the Phe-*

nomenology of the Spirit. Edited by A. Bloom. Translated by J. H. Nichols, Jr. Ithaca, N.Y.: Cornell University Press.

Lévi-Strauss, Claude. 1963. "The Sorcerer and His Magic." In his *Structural Anthropology,* translated by C. Jacobson and B. G. Schoepf, 167–185. New York: Basic Books.

Sahlins, Marshall. 1985. *Islands of History.* Chicago: University of Chicago Press.

Schneider, David M. 1968. *American Kinship.* Englewood Cliffs, N.J.: Prentice-Hall.

FIVE

On Practical Nostalgia:
Self-Prospecting among Urban
Trobrianders

Debbora Battaglia

The topic of this essay is nostalgia and its relation to postcolonial rhetorics of identity.[1] In part, my aim is critical—an outgrowth of my discomfort with the place nostalgia has come to occupy in the literatures of anthropology and cultural studies. That is, while recognizing how "nativistic nostalgia" may obscure or deny issues of social inequality (Appiah 1992), and recognizing also that Euro-American nostalgia for "tradition" and "otherness" is a dangerous motivator of scholarly quests, I shall query the assumption that nostalgia has a *categorically* negative social value for indigenous actors. In this I take a leaf from Trinh Minh-Ha[2] by suggesting that when indigenous sensibilities are taken into account, nostalgia may appear less fused to nativism and a lack of critical distance on self and the sources of cultural identity than is often presumed. Nostalgia may in fact be a vehicle of knowledge, rather than only a yearning for something lost. It may be *practiced* in diverse ways, where the issues *for users* become, on the one hand, the attachment of appropriate feelings toward their own histories, products, and capabilities, and on the other hand, their detachment from—and active resistance to—disempowering conditions of postcolonial life.

But allow me to backtrack. For it is important for my purposes here to detach the notion of nostalgia from the merely sentimental attitude with which we may too easily associate it. The nostalgia of this essay is embodied; it is the practice of yam growing for urban Trobrianders who talk about the gardens of "Home" (the Trobriand Islands) as distinct from their experience of the "house" they have returned to each day for twenty years after working "for cash" in Port Moresby. Likewise, it abides in the practices of Trobrianders fashioning identities as Papua New Guinea "nationals" on identities and entitlements, imaginary or actual, in their island homeland. I am distinguishing, then (as Marilyn Strathern notes in chap. 6 in expanding on this contrast), a nostalgia synthetic and historically modern (she cites Robertson)—a nostalgia that "mourns for what is missing from the present, and thus creates representations of the past" (Strathern, p. 111)—from what I have come to think of as a practical or active nostalgia. The latter is transformative action with a connective purpose, and the affective and aesthetic quality of an indulgence. So that Home in this construction is the excess, the luxury of experiencing an attachment to sources, which came for urban Trobrianders to be the luxury budgeted for first, before the strictly utilitarian things of life. It is in this variety that nostalgic connection may also be imagined toward a past object without necessarily being the enemy of unformulated future relationships. Indeed, nostalgia for a sense of future[3]—for an experience, however imaginary, of possessing the means of controlling the future—may function as a powerful force for social reconnection. In permitting creative lapses from dominant realities, it is such a nostalgia that enables or recalls to practice more meaningful patterns of relationship and self-action. The capacity of nostalgia to engender its own ironies is hence a central consideration here, and bears directly on how local and national cultural identities are argued and contested.

I draw the case in point from fieldwork among urban Trobrianders who were more or less permanent residents of Port Moresby in 1985. I should stress that my consultants were mainly elite Papua New Guinea "nationals"; they were not, in other words, the insular inhabitants of the Trobriands of classical ethnography. Also, the date is significant. During the harvest months that concern me here, Port Moresby was in a state of emergency in consequence of an upsurge of violent crime; the discourse of violence was pervasive in everyday conversation, in the media, in direct experience, coloring and altering the course of everyday exchanges.[4]

Against this agitated ground the event that was the focus of my inquiries stood out the more sharply—for me, and in the consciousness of its participants. This was a pioneering urban harvest competition, the First Annual Trobriand Yam Festival. In its bare outlines this event was modeled on the "competitions," or *kayasa*, at Home in the Trobriand Islands. Men had planted competitive yam gardens for prizes[5] and for later use in political exchange, in connection with a project for community enhancement sponsored by a local person of high standing. On this occasion the sponsor was John Noel, head of the National Planning and Budget office of Papua New Guinea, and a representative of the Lukuba clan. The community event was, officially, a feast, to be held in conjunction with an exhibition game of Trobriand cricket. At Noel's invitation, I was to be "the anthropologist" for the proceedings.

John Noel's vision of the event in its kayasa aspect would not allow any image of it as a salvage operation for a lost "tradition." He spoke thematically of "bringing Home to Moresby"; his stated aim was to unite the dispersed urban population, giving Trobrianders an opportunity to feel productive in their own backyards, as well as in their own cultural terms. Home, then, became (paradoxically) a rhetorical location for experiencing self-displacement in its future value as self-significance. But the valorization of displacement reached its highest expression in the event's yam festival aspect, in which John Noel foresaw Trobrianders modeling culture for all of Papua New Guinea. The dominant terrain of this latter movement was the "mediascape" (Appadurai 1990, 2) of the national press, where the Yam Festival became at one point front-page news. Now, on logical grounds, one might see the succession of levels from urbanized Trobriand to Trobriandized national identity as continuous and transcending the tensions of urban self-displacement. The rhetoric, however, could not supplant the experience of dissonant and competing modes of relationship which in fact created the distinctions: the kayasa armature was kin-based relations of alliance; the yam festival invited participants from "other ethnic groups." In short, John Noel's vision of a kayasa/festival was less effective in figuring a transcendent collectivity than in setting up an utterly artificial local/national bifocality that gave Trobrianders an experience of ambivalent tacking between the two perceived spheres of relatedness. And tensions evolved along yet another axis from the fact that the one sphere entailed mimetic performances of Trobriand selfhood in gardening, and the "fixing" or emplacement of self-images, whereas the other was serially inscribed in discursive press images and texts as a prospective or "protentive"[6] exercise—alluringly but also alarmingly open-ended. These structural and experienced tensions will orient the discussion that follows.

GARDENING AS SELF-PROBLEMATIZATION

Generations of anthropological prose suggest that for Trobriand men especially the aesthetic and political significance of gardening—the depth of the experience—is impossible to overstate. In the opening pages of *Coral Gardens and Their Magic,* Malinowski writes that Trobriand aesthetics has its roots in the garden and in "things which promise safety, prosperity, abundance and sensual pleasure"; that Trobrianders "would agree with Stendhal's definition of beauty as the promise of bliss, rather than with Kant's emasculated statement about disinterested contemplation as the essence of aesthetic enjoyment" (1965 [1935], vol. 1, p. 10).

Certainly, there was nothing "disinterested" about Trobriand gardening as I observed it in Port Moresby. Yet, too, the notion of "bliss" captures the romance but perhaps not the *directed movement* in feeling that urban gardening precipitated and revealed as cultural nostalgia. Listen to the words of some of the major participants:

> *Charles Lepani:* Sometimes a man works in a store. He gets paid but his paycheck is already spent, and he is hungry. Then he can go to the garden. He looks out over the yams growing and he feels full. Just watching the garden he feels satisfied.

> *Geoffrey Masuwadoga:* If you can make the object [a reference here to a yam or some other exchange item] part of you through experience, it takes on meaning. You can romanticize about the garden. Then you make the garden and you find why this [n.b.: the romance? the garden? both?] is important. That experience becomes your personality which you cannot just wipe away.

> *John Noel:* Home is Kilivila, even if you're born here. Nostalgia pulls you back to the place (*valu*). At the office I'll say I'm going to the house, not home. In Port Moresby, you get a sense of valu by making gardens. You've lifted the land and brought it here. It's what you *do* to make it your land that gives you that feeling.

In these passages, very powerful feelings of sufficiency, significance, and empowerment are given as the immediate outcome of making a place for gardens *within* one's experience of the present. To the extent that gardening, as represented in its products, is internalized (this is arguably a significant tropeic displacement; men grow yams to give them away in exchange and not to eat them themselves), it accomplishes an aesthetic and political *supplementation*. A man is *more* for gardening—experiences more *of* himself and his relational capacity; is in his person more culturally located. Yams, then, as much grow their subjects as the other way around. Gardeners trade on their ability to embody supplementation, incorporating others in exchanges that expand their own political parameters. Thus the gardening experience is transformed and structured as a historical significance, outward from the site of the gardener it functions to transform.

For Trobrianders I knew, this significance lay in their regard for yams not as natural things but as personal and cultural projects. Yams were not automatic products of mechanical practices; rather, the relation of product to producer was sensitive and problematic. For example, at the level of gardening skill it was held that the size of the yield was commensurate with the effectiveness of the gardener's magic. Such things as the area of garden plots and the quality of the soil and weather conditions were taken into account, but the magic factor prevailed in explanations of the outcome. Yams' shapes gave hints as to the kind of magic the gardener had used: for example, dolphin magic (dolphin imagery in the spell) was a *prerequisite* of producing the graceful effect of gently arcing yams; the gardener's personal hygiene and attention to appearance were prerequisites for producing healthy, attractive yams. Because persons were seen as shaping or influencing material forms that made their intentions and qualities apparent, such forms were read as the traces of this capacity of the gardener—of the quality of his social being. Thus, yams were said literally to shrink from displays of temper, from body odor, and so forth, all traceable to flaws in the gardener, to his "bad *character*" (as I heard it said). A yam that was split during harvesting might be given as proof of mental distraction (most often attributed to domestic discord). Likewise, the malevolent intent of others could intervene to prevent yams from growing as they should, or where they should: a jealous or competitive person's magic could block the growth of yams or induce them to wander from the garden where they were planted, and stunted yams or small yields were seen as possible evidence of this.

Urban circumstances made gardening even more problematic. Indeed, the deepest sense to be made of urban gardening may well be as a "practice of self-problematization" (to take a phrase Ian Hunter uses to define the work of art [1992, 348]). The sponsor, for example, while highly placed in the national government, was a "Bau man": a person of legendary low rank within the Trobriand system of ranked matrilineages. It was Bau ancestors who brought lethal magic to the Trobriand Islands, and who embodied opposition to the noble chiefly lineages and their magic for controlling growth and abundance. The image of the sponsor as an "urban chief" was anomalous—and politically charged. As harvesting drew to a close, "Bau jokes" surfaced in Port Moresby, jokes that featured stereotypically, sometimes dangerously foolish figures doing things "upside down" (see Battaglia 1992). John Noel's act of leadership was to some Trobrianders liberating and revolutionary, to others preposterous. Basically, the impact of his self-destabilization was due to his use of a postcolonial rhetoric of independence—John Noel once called himself an "urban cowboy"—a rhetoric supplemental to the subversion the Bau man embodied as the "joke" belying the Trobriand myth of a stable, given order of rank and power. So that when Geri Tokilivila, a cosmopolitan of chiefly lineage, announced that he would be "gardening for" John Noel, Trobrianders in town and at Home became fixated on his decision. The action of encouraging Noel's anomalous self-action, as it were, from the top down of inherited status, was for many indexical of the disruptive effect of the urban-Bau phenomenon.

Then, too, disruptions were occurring at other sites of self-action, within a wholly collective, relational rhetoric. From the start, Trobriand gardeners had conceived of the yam competition as a kind of mission to disprove that "yams won't grow in Moresby soil"—something "everyone in Port Moresby" knew. The mission originated in a challenge John Noel had issued to rally their support for the competition in the early stages. It also echoed a mythic precedent in which the first agriculturalist-hero of the Trobriands struck out on an odyssey, selflessly risking great dangers, bringing Trobriand yams and a knowledge of agriculture to foreign lands. The heroic challenge was to replicate growth in a hostile environment,[7] or more precisely to control replicaton along the lines of productive gardening at Home. Yet defining urban gardening in this way as a demonstration for "everybody" in town who had gardened there in the past cast their competition as a direct challenge to non-Trobrianders, who needless to say took a different view of the enterprise.

These rhetorics conjoined and were distilled in the sponsor's founding vision that gardening would be, for Trobrianders everywhere, a kayasa that would "bring Home to Moresby," but also an event-commodity for a paying, culturally heterogeneous urban public. However, the conjunction confounded a critically important imaginary order for Trobrianders in which "working for yams" and "working for money" were separate "games," with different and opposing evaluative premises. Urban Trobrianders relied on the categorical separation of these "games" for justifying the compromises they made in each sphere: on one level, to deny the opposition was to deny the tensions urban gardeners experienced as, for the most part, full-time wage earners who also had ongoing debt-based relationships to kin at Home and in town. And it was their experiences of these very tensions that caused Trobriand gardeners to embrace this particular form of practical nostalgia in Port Moresby. By producing yams, the coin of debt-based relationality, they supplemented the cash they were unable to stretch to that end.

The urban competition acknowledged tensions arising from the coterminous practice of gift and commodity *scales* of exchange[8] by dividing gardens into "backyard" and "long-distance" for the purpose of judging their yields. On the one hand, this displacement in fact mitigated tension by recognizing the incomparability of the smaller inner city gardens to the larger, in some cases commercial, fields Trobrianders planted outside the city limits. Reframing the distinction between kayasa and yam festival, the effect was to cast these as complementary rather than antagonistically linked processes. On the other hand, and perhaps more significantly, the distinction officially inscribed status asymmetries in terms of access to transport: one had to own a vehicle, for urban Trobrianders the quintessential sign of self and status mobility, in order to work and manage long-distance gardens. In many respects cars and pickup trucks were indeed the commodity equivalents of deep-sea canoes used at Home in the long-distance exchange politics of the "kula game."[9] In town, however, political self-extension was cast as fundamentally individuating and open-ended, on the model of the open-ended convertibility of commodity exchange. As such, it existed in tension with the finite convertibility of perishable yams into social relations through acts of giving and indebtedness. It also existed in tension with the indigenous poetics of replicating growth, since the ready-made quality of commodities substituted the purchase of products for the experience of meaningful productivity.[10]

Yam Displays and the Ethnographic Present

The potential of commoditization to overwhelm, perhaps even to appropriate, nostalgic practice became evident *as an indigenous problematic* in the context of yam display, which, as we shall observe, was dedicated at every turn to denying commoditization this potential. The situation generated an interesting problem of ethnography, having to do with Trobriand subjects' concerns that I, "the anthropologist" who had never set foot in the Trobriand Islands, understand their garden displays, which they viewed as emblematic of their efforts in the urban competition but basically substandard. Gardeners were in some cases insistent that I record, on the spot, how things ought properly to be done by describing to me how they were done at Home. And so I was conscripted into my subjects' "theatre of fact" (Wagner 1986, 99) in my function for them of *implementing their nostalgia;* a function that involved me in giving voice to their argument that they were more competent as gardeners than their urban yields would indicate.

I was told, then: At Home, freshly harvested yams "are" (note the ethnographic present) washed, in some cases painted (if the garden is a chief's or if the yield is pledged to a chief), and arranged for display beneath a simple lean-to shelter at the garden perimeter. The shelter protects the yams from rain. Individual short yams are arranged in a conical stack, large clusters of "mother yams and offsprings" are hung from the shelter supports, and long yams are displayed in stick frames. The gardenside display draws casual observers who may also be shopping *(vem)* for next year's seed, and at some point the host of the kayasa visits the site on his circuit of gardenside yields to be measured and judged. The host observes the hanging yams and measures the stack around the base, using a string. The same string is used to measure all of the stacks on the village or hamlet circuit. Small flags mark the different circumferences, placing the yields relative to one another along a line when the string is displayed. Prizes are awarded based on this measurement, which is expressed in terms of armspread-lengths. Clusters and long yams merit separate and smaller prizes. Thus, yam displays are an index of the industry, skill, and social strength of the gardener and his support group of workers, those who garden "for" him.

The shape of the conical stack indicates the skill of a stacker, often an expert of the gardener's paternal or maternal matrician, who must project the correct dimensions for the base from the number, sizes, and shapes of the yams; must then arrange the yams so that the stack is stable; and must manage not to end up accidentally with a stack like an onion-shaped dome (my association)—which in most regions of the Trobriands is viewed as a form of resume expansion. In the islands, garden yields run to seven armspreads. Prize-winning displays in Port Moresby would run to only four—a nearly child-sized yield by island standards—a "joke" *(koila)* in the gardeners' own assessments. This joke was for some merely an aside to the larger "joke" *(sopa)*, more serious and even actionable in traditional courts, of a "Bau man" standing for Trobriand culture in the national capital and conducting himself as an "urban chief" (for more on the Bau man stereotype and John Noel's strategic vision, see Battaglia 1992).

But I digress from material issues about which there is much more to say. For example, yam displays in Port Moresby were visited not once but several times by persons professing to be, or to be acting for, "the real" authorities, using "the real" string that the sponsor would be using to determine the prize winners. (My witnessing this practice led one man to joke that my presence in Port Moresby threatened to keep the judging honest.) A major point of the exercise became apparent at these moments as the social exchange for which the objects provided a material location and some thematic coherence. Subjective evaluations of the yam displays on these occasions often reflected the state of relations between gardener and critic as much or more than the objective qualities of the yams or of the gardener's domestic scene, and critics appeared not in the least disconcerted by this.

Also, in town, yams grown from Trobriand seed and acquired from relatives were valued over seed that was purchased in the market from non-Trobriand growers, although market yams may have been finer and much admired in other contexts. On this score the aesthetic point conveyed an explicitly ethical one: commodities were no substitute for the yams one produced from inherited seed, an investment in labor, and the inducement of magical words. Thus displays tended to be arranged so that the smaller, scarred, nonlocal or market yams were stacked on the inside, not visible to observers. In other words, such yams—and the character flaws they evinced—were *denied* in the visual rhetoric of display, rather than simply left out as (gardeners indicated) they might have been at Home. This practice was directly related to the small quantity of yams available in town. But it also calls attention to displays as concrete arguments of a particular model of identity.

Now, the ethics of display stipulate that stacking be done only once, immediately after the harvesting is completed. The work is to take place at the garden as I have indicated, such that there is one display per garden owner. In Port Moresby gardenside displays were not practical, particularly for long-distance gardens; thieves would have made off with the harvest (and people joked that thieves "helped with the harvest" often enough). Instead, individual yams were packed carefully in leaves to minimize jostling and loaded into cars and pickup trucks, then driven to the residential yards of their owners for stacking. This practice, opening up as it did opportunities for creative intervention, drew intense critical scrutiny. The general opinion was that the yields of several persons' gardens had in some cases been combined prior to stacking and measuring. Discerning critics reported traces of red Trobriand earth on yams in backyard displays (I must say that I was at a loss to detect it), establishing the final destination of large and costly shipments of Trobriand yams spotted at the national airport. Suspicions ran high along these lines when yam displays were disassembled and restacked, as noted by competitors cruising the displays in their cars at all hours of the day, and at night up to the time of curfew.

Listening to participants in the days of stacking as yam-centric discourse proliferated, one got the impression of furious cosmetic reconstruction of the yam displays, serving an uncontrolled expansion of unorthodox social contracts. Basically, displays were growing at a time when growth ought to have ceased. The situation contradicted their function as monumental forms, iconic of a job well *done* as much as of plenitude. It was as if the space-time open-endedness of modern transportation vehicles (e.g., cars, trucks, airplanes), uncontrolled consumption (e.g., of thieves), and unprecedented partnerships (e.g., chiefs who gardened for commoners) were inhabiting the yam displays.

On the Paradox of Decorated Yam Shelters

At Home, a stack of yams is disassembled after measuring and the yams are removed from the shelter site and delivered to a person or persons as a substantive statement of political support. The recipients are typically married sisters (the yams are for passing along electively to their husbands), village or hamlet headmen, and/or chiefs. The yams from various supporters are combined in the recipient's yam house. There they constitute a form of publicity of the extent of his support base, a visible rendering of his centrality and that of his wife relative to others who in effect have created it. Yams donated by a person of rank or intended for a person of rank are decorated with the appropriate designs and accoutrements either before or after merging with the yams of others. The recipient's yam house is decorated, *but not the donors' yam shelters,* with insignia of rank.

In Port Moresby, only one yam house was built and decorated (by the highest-ranking male in town, a Tabalu lineage person of the Malasi clan). Other gardeners chose not to build proper yam houses, wishing, they said, to avoid embarrassing themselves or their supporters by predicting or exhibiting the meager yam support that could be mustered in town. However, certain men chose to displace their statements of rank (established or rhetorical) onto their yam shelters.

The significance of this action is given by the clue that unlike yam houses, the yam shelters of Home are not decorated. Now, on this subject I lack detailed exegesis from urban consultants and accordingly depart into published ethnography, where it is written that insignia of rank traditionally attach to the person of the recipient not so much as an individual, but rather as an instantiation of past and future coherence for asymmetrical relationships (Weiner 1976, 215)—relationships that culminate in the practice of rank and the display of its insignia. Another way of putting this is that a person and his decorated yam house *orient a consciousness* of status asymmetry. And as such, they make apparent what the recipient as an individual masks, namely, the superordination of those values and the material dividuality—the historical contingency—of social relations. Thus, persons could choose not to display the insignia to which they were entitled by birth or inheritance but instead to allow them to remain latent—the term I heard was "submerged"—until such time as their own social support base was strong enough to warrant display.

A yam house, then, is (quoting Weiner) a "personification . . . symbolizing the power of a man who knows how to make relationships work . . . [of] past and future relationships . . . which . . . *aggrandizes the continuity of those relationships*" (1976, 214–215; emphasis mine). By contrast, the shelter substitutes of Port Moresby embodied a destabilized, culturally qualified social continuity. Upon these traditional structures for attempting fresh starts—structures attached to the garden and the gardener only for the growing season—the insignia of rank rested very tentatively; the heavy weight of inherited status and rhetorical claims to rank (e.g., a fourth coconut-husk wedge where only three were prescribed) rocking the supports of urban relationships. In short, the value of rank was in town displayed as temporary and context-specific—and ironically, was thus more congruent with urban realities and the kind of emergent rhetoric of individuality that allowed John Noel to refer to himself as an urban cowboy. Visual hedges against an order of rank that was virtually unpracticable and possibly even undesirable, these shelters were more *prefigurations* (borrowing here from Brenkman [1987] on the nature of political prefiguration) [11] than culminations of social relationships.

So far, I have tried to convey something of the value of Home for urban Trobrianders—its idealized and pleasantly ahistorical fields of right conduct. I have shown how the notion of Home is basically emergent in its function of establishing a stable point of return for Trobrianders constructing nostalgic futures for identities *in the course of their participation in ethnography.* I have also indicated how yam cultivation and display were a means of bringing subjects into being in the terms of an aesthetic discourse that objectified moral and ethical dimensions of contemporary social life. I have detailed some of the ways in which subjects' powers of self-reconfiguration, embellishment, and redaction were revealed in the urban contingencies of yam displays; and how displays served as a "site for individuals to begin to relate to themselves as subjects of aesthetic experience" (Hunter 1992, 348). Reframed in the embodied nostalgia of the urban yam competition, these practices made apparent the capacity of nostalgia to engender, on the one hand, a "joke" of identity and, on the other, aesthetic experiences of self. But these divergent courses had only just begun to play out at gardens and sites of social action when a new tool of identity making became suddenly fashionable.

"PUBLICITY"

The rhetoric of self-making took an intriguing turn when pictures of Trobriand yams began appearing in the national press. Trobrianders invariably spoke of the press coverage—photographs, reportage, and editorials—as "publicity." For some, the publicity was seen as a rhetorical tool of elite sponsors fashioning themselves as traditional by drawing attention to Trobriand culture. The sponsors, meanwhile, claimed an altruistic motive: publicity served a valuable connective function to other Papua New Guinea nationals.

With this conversation in mind, I turn now to consider a day in the life of Trobriand publicity, June 6, 1985, beginning with the front page of the *Niu-*

gini Nius. A tabloid-size photograph shows a little boy holding a large yam and scowling into the camera. The child is dressed for soccer and wears a Trobriand-style necklace. The copy reads:

> Something is cooking and young Nathaniel Mwasisibuyagu Lepani is digging in to find out. And after a hard day's work he deserves to be rewarded with this bunch of his dad, Charles' food garden harvest near Port Moresby. It looks yummy! Find out more on page 3. Mwasisibuyagu means Elated Gardener.

Sharing the front page with Mwasisibuyagu are (top story) the decision of the Coffee Industry Association to impose an indefinite ban on buying coffee on the roads in two Highlands provinces in consequence of "armed hold-ups, fraud and murder within the coffee industry and around the nation," a call by the leader of the opposition to investigate the association of high government officials with drug-running activities, a photograph of young boys begging in a middle-class district of Port Moresby (coincidentally the same district where little Elated Gardener lived in comparative affluence). And there is an ad for biscuits.

We turn to page 3 and another large photograph. Foregrounded is an orderly display of yams, each one painted with a white circle; behind them, a man in traditional Trobriand dress and ornaments holds up a very large yam. The headline reads "Trobriand Yams Galore," and the text

> The yam season is on in the Trobriand Islands and here in Port Moresby Trobriand Islanders are also in the festive mood. They have begun harvesting yams for a yam competition next month. Charles Lepani who owns a farm outside Port Moresby has a yam garden and a chief gardener, Uta Tom (above) who has started harvesting his yams. Mr. Lepani said he brought the seedlings from the Trobriand Islands and planted the first lot in October last year.

Stories on the same page: the prime minister's defense of his comment that the nation's capital was "filthy" and that residents "had no self-respect"; the Roman Catholic archbishop of Port Moresby speaking out against the death penalty; speculation that an acute shortage of engineers had led to explosive decompression in an Air Niugini F28; a defamation suit brought against two national newspapers by Pel Air in connection with the drug-related search of one of Pel Air's aircraft; a statement by the prime minister that crime posed "the greatest threat" to Papua New Guinea, in which he stresses that agricultural development is the backbone for Papua New Guinea's future growth; an ad for Gourmet Night at the Islander Hotel.

I offer these texts not simply as postmodern pastiche but to indicate the general context of the Trobriand print images, and the national readership the frame of the page presumed and solicited. The social life of "publicity" derived partly from its effect of bifocalizing[12] national and subnational place attachments to Home and to Town. This bifocality, mapped iconically in the layout of the printed page, replayed the sponsor's vision of (self-) extension. Meanwhile, however, Trobrianders discerned other messages in the texts and images, including most controversially the invisible influence of Charles Lepani, who was father to the child, employer (and paternal nephew) to the gardener, and a member of the sponsoring Bau matrilineage. The images linked Lepani to indigenous modes of productivity and traditional emblems of relationship: foregrounded were his paternal identifications: his status as father to his son and as "father" to his yams, and his effort to establish identification with his own father's chiefly lineage. They also suggested an image of Lepani as a chief: the yam decorations were traditionally the mark of chiefly rank. In short, we observe an explicit rhetoric of *self-prospecting in the direction of paternal sources.* Significantly absent or underplayed in the "publicity" were references to Lepani's own maternal (Bau) matrilineage, and to his cosmopolitan identity (e.g., Lepani had a Harvard M.P.A., a place in history as the first head of the National Planning and Budget office for Papua New Guinea, and his own international consulting business). In overall effect, the Lepani who was present in absentia in the newspaper text was a retrograde fiction, nostalgically but also pragmatically distanced from problematic cosmopolitan and kin-based identifications. But once again, to high-ranked Trobrianders the painted yams suggested that elite commoners were presenting themselves as chiefs in town. The irony was that Uta the gardener, not Charles Lepani, had decided to decorate the yams and to pose beside them for the photographers, out of respect, he said, for Lepani as an "urban chief." Further, the photo session had been arranged by Lepani initially on what was clearly theatrical impulse as he and I were discussing the yam festival in his office. An enormous controversy ensued that included threats of sorcery and poisoning by Trobriand chiefs and their allies at Home and in town. Lepani, who on one level enjoyed being seen in this context as inflammatory—who was fundamentally ambivalent about his role in the yam festival—had sparked the machinery of reproduction by inviting reporters to his garden. But his paternal uncle had dispatched the political profile that Trobrianders said "made people talk," that gave the story an *ongoing* interest-value.

From these exchanges was generated—more publicity! This included a feature story in the Sunday *Times* travel supplement on the enduring glory of the chiefs of Kiriwina, and competitive photographs of a young Trobriand cohost posing with his long yam and a Sepik Member of Parliament with his even longer one, and eventually, a photograph of me taking notes beside a yam display.

If we accept that language has the power to constitute that which it represents, newspaper images of yams—in which Trobrianders "read" selected features of their gardeners—accomplished the making of gardeners' images no
less as copies than the yam displays did as sites of cultural authenticity. However, as the content of the publicity was as much a product of audience speculation, chance intervention, and the anthropologist's engagement, as of the
sponsors' design—as it was *heterogeneously* coauthored—the nondeterminative nature (see Bourdieu 1977; Giddens 1984) and structural ironies of nostalgic production (see Marcus 1986 and chap. 3, this volume) were more
salient in publicity than in the homogeneously authored yam displays. Also,
the ethical concerns articulated as aesthetic judgments in yam displays revealed the degree to which Trobrianders were invested in the myth and value
of image *stability*. The infinite replicability of images that newspapers permitted, and the fact of journalistic agency, gave a value to the *mobility* of images.
This value subverted the operating premise of the gardening competition
that the concrete image of the yield was indexical of a gardener's skill and
influence. And it subverted the myth of Home as a point of reference for all
that was authentic.

One effect of this expansive mediation was that Trobriand subjects became
newly distanced on themselves and their yam self-objects. I venture to say
that it was not coincidental that as nostalgic, internalizing practices were
picked up in the press as "yam festival" for display to a mass audience, critics
of the event became more vocal. The Bau men, I heard, were "making a
spectacle of themselves" and of Trobriand culture. The sponsors were not
behaving "with dignity . . . you know, the British understatement"—this
from a high-ranking person (who incidentally was himself a notorious con
man on an international scale with a long history of political opposition to
certain of the key figures, including Charles Lepani). Speculation intensified
about the "true" motive for the attention getting. As urban Trobrianders
became actively engaged (and engaged me) in this detective work, a dual
hypothesis emerged that the hosts were seeking a route back to a political
future in their Trobriand homeland (e.g., that John Noel was preparing to
seek elected office and needed to heighten his profile among his electorate)
and an escape route from the grip of Port Moresby's "cash economy." Ironically, then, it was the trumpeting of praise for Trobriand cultural practice
that enabled chiefly critics of the sponsor and his lineagemates to "re-cover"
(following Donald Weber [n.d.], I use the verb to suggest the effect of "historical shrouding") a wide-ranging critical voice.

But beyond matters of form, some held that the publicity was literally
dangerous. Urban Trobrianders talked about fearing the effect of their cultural event being cast as a model for other cultures or for a national culture.

Some recalled the ethnic violence surrounding a national court case six years earlier, when wearing a Trobriand-style necklace could provoke an attack by Highlanders considerably larger physically and in numbers. Some were concerned that jealous magicians might try to spoil yams displayed so ostentatiously in the press. In short, to be successful in Trobriand terms, the publicity would have to elicit an active nostalgia for meaningful productivity without being taken as modeling culture for all Papua New Guineans.

Consider in this light the text of the editorial that appeared in the June 6 issue of the *Niugini News*, titled "A Culture To Be Proud Of":

> Little things contribute to bigger and better things. . . . [One] tradition which is shaping up in Port Moresby is the Trobriand Islands yam festival. It is a first-ever event to be staged in the National Capital and has drawn a wide interest not just from the Milne Bay community but also other culture-minded Papua New Guineans. The promotion of culture both within and without the country should be actively encouraged by the Government through its relevant department. We should be proud of our culture—it is second to none and it is very much alive. Yet most times we seem to forget this.

In this text, we witness an interesting effect of supplementary agency, as an editor appropriates images of the original act of appropriation (wherein local objects were employed in asserting local identities) for the purpose of incorporating these into a national identity. In other words, what might be seen as the unmaking of a national identity in the first set of "publicity" photographs becomes, ironically, part of a composite picture for use in remaking national cultural identity in the editorial.

When I first came across this piece I was incapable of reading it uncritically. I saw in the message a kind of postmodern animism: culture is "alive" because it exhibits movement across levels of society and boundaries of culture. Yet it seemed that this movement of culture-things (yams, performances, or whatever) uprooted them from their historicity; from a social space and time to which practitioners continued to refer their significance. "Culture" was also for this editor endangered, easily forgotten, or abandoned. Export it to Port Moresby, give it a friendly environment in the boiler room of nationalism and some incentive to reproduce, and perhaps this small transplant (standing in a part-for-whole relation to a properly integrated national culture) would even be discovered to have value as a commodity. But note: the government had been deficient in its function of commodifying culture (on this general theme, see the discussion in Foster 1991). It had been deficient as (quoting Clifford 1986, 113) the "recorder and interpreter of fragile custom . . . [the] unimpeachable witness to an authenticity"—in other words, as a "moral authority." "The allegory of salvage is deeply ingrained" indeed (Clifford 1986, 113), but it is ingrained in contemporary ethnographic practice less vividly than in the rhetoric of national cultural identity reinvented with confounding innocence—but also exemplary high purpose—by sophisticated indigenes (e.g., the mythically coherent Papua New Guinea "culture" was "second to none"). Thus, the editorial story, while running against the grain of innocent nostalgia for Trobrianders, effectivly recovered the romance and the innocence to a project of imaging nationalism. This romantic invention of a national culture—a culture on the model of authentic "cultures" it would export—reconfigured the gift-commodity relationship once again.[13]

Overall, however much Trobrianders sought to dehistoricize and distinguish Trobriand culture, removing it both from a continuous and homogeneous national past (see Anderson 1983) and from the "cash economy"; however strikingly they cast their cultural activity as inwardly and not outwardly competitive, their readership and unsolicited coauthors defeated them. Exhibiting what Arjun Appadurai has termed a "paradox of constructed primordialism" (Appadurai 1990, 2), the "mediascape" betrayed a dangerous ambiguity, an unruliness. Because the publicity was both a "potential resolution shape" *of* existing relations of power (I cite Lave 1988) and a prefigurement *for* the realignment of political relations *on an unknowable scale,* it promised to impact on social discourse beyond the parameters of the yam competition. Indeed, the prospective or protensive dimension was for Trobrianders the salient characteristic of publicity—and what made it a matter of critical concern. For as the print readership was drawn from different spheres of relationship as defined by scale (e.g., national and subnational), the significance of publicity and the effects on social relations of its images and texts were not fixed at any one time or place. In this respect press publicity was fundamentally different from the indigenous self-display of the shelters and stacks, although yams were featured items in all of these. As the publicity traveled in place of persons in newspaper delivery vehicles and on the legs of vendors and the buying public, it soon became apparent that it had acquired a life of its own which trailed Trobriand futures in its wake. The rhetorics of individuality and collectivity could not, in such a situation, hope to hold their relative boundaries. And so the quest for identity in the cultural imaginary proceeded locally and nationally in tandem but at cross-purposes, led on by the modest grass-roots image of the yam.

IN CONCLUSION

The discourse of mimicry is constructed around an ambivalence; in order to be effective, mimicry must continually produce its slippage, its excess, its difference.

—HOMI BHABHA

I have argued that nostalgia does not invariably entail false contact that subverts "authentic" engagement; is not for Trobriand subjects merely a yearning for some real or authentic thing. Rather, it generates a sense of productive engagement which is at once more personal and larger than any product it might find as its object. As cultural practice, then, it abides in a convergence of mimesis and poesis—in acts of replicating the social conditions of and for feeling, such that one's experience of social life is supplemented and qualitatively altered. The rupture from present conduct permitted by this social action of *extension toward sources* opens subjects to creative reconfiguration: nostalgic practice invites self-problematization. It follows that any notion of an integral, coherent self—any value universally applied to such—must be seriously reconsidered, together with any notion that an aesthetic of self-wholeness or completeness extends in practice across cultures and times.

Linda Hutcheon has written that nostalgia "connotes evasion of the present, idealization of a (fantasy) past, or a recovery of that past as edenic. . . . [An] ironic rethinking of history is definitely not nostalgic [since] it critically confronts the past with the present, and vice versa" (1988, 39). But in the Trobriand context nostalgic practice, partly in confronting the forces of commoditization, partly by engaging "the anthropologist," as well as by other means not touched upon here, reinvented the present, engendering structural ironies (as well as moments of self-realization) at every turn in its social life. As such it created not a representation of tradition but rather a "gap" (as Bhabha discusses it [1990]) in which alternative, cohabiting identities could become apparent as elements in elite actors' urban self-prospecting. The situation does not permit discussion in terms of an exclusively sentimental, disembodied affect, although the gap, as an indulgence, invites a different formulation of the risks this argument runs for urban than for locally based practitioners.

Indeed, I am suggesting that practitioners of nostalgia, "lapsing" into it, may thereby come to realize a productive capacity. Before we speak critically of nostalgia in blanket terms, we must recognize that negative or positive judgments about the appropriate use of nostalgia have the quality of aesthetic judgments, and as such inscribe political positions it is important to locate. To be trapped within a negative, disembodied concept of nostalgia is to preclude appreciation of nostalgia as a vehicle for knowledge and experience with a culturally specific historicity and a wholly *contingent* aesthetic efficacy. It is precisely because nostalgia has power to reposition within the present those who engage it that its positive and negative values for users must be closely monitored in their historicity. As we come to explore the reconfigurations of self that nostalgic practice permits or obstructs, the memories it instantiates, and the forgetting it allows or abets, its implications for subjects occupying multiple sites in culture and in history become apparent, and our efforts to capture "the contingency of the aesthetic" (Hunter 1992, 358) in postcolonial situations become, I suggest, worthwhile.

NOTES

1. The writing of this essay was made possible by a National Endowment for the Humanities fellowship and by grants from Mount Holyoke College. I am grateful to George Marcus for calling attention to the role of the ethnographer in nostalgic productivity. My conversations with Marilyn Strathern, her insights into what she terms "substantive" nostalgia, have had their usual inspiring effect (to an end I take responsibility for entirely). I am also appreciative of the comments of Julie Taylor, Stuart Kirsch, and Jimmy Weiner on earlier versions of this chapter.

2. She writes, "Even in this age of 'decolonization' one frequently encounters situations where the white man still arrogates the privilege to tell Third World individuals, *without any hesitation or consideration* . . . that they are nostalgic or naive toward their own culture" (1987, 139; emphasis mine).

3. I am reminded of Michael Fischer's comment that ethnic memory is—he said "ought to be"—future and not past oriented (1986, 196).

4. I wish to emphasize here that this essay derives from a historical moment of national crisis in Papua New Guinea. Accordingly, I take the position that while these conditions, and undoubtedly the everyday experiences of Port Moresby urbanites, have changed considerably, the social facts described here remain a point of significant reference in the ongoing transformations and reproductions of urban Trobriand historicity.

5. These prizes were announced as including cash, a pig, and a stone ax blade. For discussion of the ax blade's significance in this context, see Battaglia 1993.

6. I would refer readers of Melanesian ethnography to important extensions of Husserl's notion of protension in Munn 1990 and Weiner 1991.

7. See Battaglia 1992 for a brief discussion of the heroics of gardening in the myth of Tudava-Gerehu.

8. This is a problematic addressed recently by Strathern 1991, a study of scale and proportion in anthropological comparison. I would note in particular her premise that different social orders of complexity cannot be compared (p. 23); that "pluralities have their own configurations," such that people relate to global diversity in different ways (p. 21).

9. For a wonderful discussion of the "poetics of cars" in east Africa, see Weiss, forthcoming.

10. Here I am indebted to Weiss's complex discussion of Haya commoditization, in which he comments that

> commoditization, with its easy convertibility of objects, especially alters the spatio-temporal connectivities between persons and things which are generated through work, cultivation, inheritance, affinity, and other generative activities . . . Commoditization provides tangible evidence of the plenitude of possibilities that is characteristic of modernity, a situation in which the total procedures of production and circulation are largely unknown, and to that degree uncontrollable. (forthcoming, 240–241)

11. Christensen writes of this connection, referring to Brenkman's use of prefiguration "to characterize the performance of a political intention that was real but never fully realized, that may have been put to the service of [a particular ideology or order of practice] but that was not [that ideology or practice] itself" (1990, 449).

12. For a rich and pertinent discussion of bifocalization, see Gupta and Fergusson 1992.

13. This is a reflection of the premise, evident in the choice of subject here and in other Papua New Guinea media such as video, that "the urban cultural mix allegorizes the country" (Sullivan 1991, 4). The editorial suggests that "culture" and "development" can live and travel together only if the former (a reification) is pressed into service of the latter (a process). By denying culture its status as process—vis-à-vis development, a subversive force to be reckoned with—the rhetorical stance of the editorial depotentiated that which it would valorize.

REFERENCES

Anderson, Benedict. 1983. *Imagined Communities: Reflections on the Origin and Spread of Nationalism*. London: Verso.

Appadurai, Arjun. 1990. "Disjuncture and Difference in the Global Cultural Economy." *Public Culture* 2:1–24.

Appiah, Kwame Anthony. 1992. *In My Father's House*. Oxford: Oxford University Press.

Battaglia, D. 1992. "Displacing Culture: A Joke of Significance in Urban Papua New Guinea." *New Literary History* 23:1003–1017.

———. 1993. "Retaining Reality: Some Practical Problems with Objects as Property." Paper for the session on Visual Representation and Systems of Visual Knowledge, Association for Social Anthropology decennial meetings, Oxford University, July.

Bhabha, Homi. 1990. "On Mimicry and Man: The Ambivalence of Colonial Discourse." *October* 28:125–133.

Bourdieu, Pierre. 1977. *Outline of a Theory of Practice*. Cambridge: Cambridge University Press.

Brenkman, John. 1987. *Culture and Domination*. Ithaca, N.Y.: Cornell University Press.

Christensen, Jerome. 1990. "From Rhetoric to Corporate Populism: A Romantic Critique of the Academy in an Age of High Gossip." *Critical Inquiry* 16:438–465.

Clifford, James. 1986. "On Ethnographic Allegory." In *Writing Culture: The Poetics and Politics of Ethnography*, edited by J. Clifford and G. Marcus, 98–121. Berkeley, Los Angeles, London: University of California Press.

Clifford, James, and George Marcus, eds. 1986. *Writing Culture: The Poetics and Politics of Ethnography*. Berkeley, Los Angeles, London: University of California Press.

Fischer, Michael. 1986. "Ethnicity and the Post-modern Arts of Memory." In *Writing Culture: The Poetics and Politics of Ethnography*, edited by J. Clifford and G. Marcus, 194–233. Berkeley, Los Angeles, London: University of California Press.

Foster, Robert. 1991. "Making National Cultures in the Global Ecumene." *Annual Review of Anthropology* 20:235–260.

Giddens, Anthony. 1984. *The Constitution of Society: Outline of the Theory of Structuration.* Berkeley, Los Angeles, London: University of California Press.

Gupta, Akhil, and James Fergusson. 1992. "Beyond 'Culture': Space, Identity, and the Politics of Difference." *Cultural Anthropology* 7:6–23.

Hunter, Ian. 1992. "Aesthetics and Cultural Studies." In *Cultural Studies,* edited by Lawrence Grossberg, Cary Nelson, and Paula Treichler, 347–367. New York: Routledge.

Hutcheon, Linda. 1988. *A Poetics of Postmodernism: History, Theory, Fiction.* New York: Routledge.

Lave, J. 1988. *Cognition in Practice: Mind, Mathematics, and Culture.* Cambridge: Cambridge University Press.

Malinowski, Bronislaw K. 1965 [1935]. *Coral Gardens and Their Magic: A Study of the Methods of Tilling the Soil and of Agricultural Rites in the Trobriand Islands.* Vols. 1 and 2. Bloomington: Indiana University Press.

Marcus, George. 1986. "Contemporary Problems of Ethnography in the Modern World System." In *Writing Culture: The Poetics and Politics of Ethnography,* edited by J. Clifford and G. Marcus, 165–193. Berkeley, Los Angeles, London: University of California Press.

Minh-Ha, Trinh. 1987. "Of Other Peoples: Beyond the Salvage Paradigm." In *Discussions in Contemporary Culture,* edited by Hal Foster, 138–141. Seattle: Bay Press.

Munn, Nancy. 1990. "Constructing Regional Worlds in Experience: Kula Exchange, Witchcraft, and Gawan Local Events." *Man* (n.s.) 25:1–17.

Strathern, Marilyn. 1991. *Partial Connections.* Savage, Md.: Rowman and Littlefield.

Sullivan, Nancy. 1991. "Indigenous Media in Papua New Guinea." Paper presented at the American Anthropological Association meeting, Chicago, November 20–24.

Wagner, Roy. 1986. "The Theater of Fact and Its Critics." *Anthropological Quarterly* 59:97–99.

Weber, Donald. n.d. "Repression and Memory in Early Ethnic Television." Manuscript. Mount Holyoke College, South Hadley, Mass.

Weiner, Annette. 1976. *Women of Value, Men of Renown: New Perspectives in Trobriand Exchange.* Austin: University of Texas Press.

Weiner, James. 1991. *The Empty Place: Poetry, Space, and Being among the Foi of Papua New Guinea.* Bloomington and Indianapolis: Indiana University Press.

Weiss, Brad. Forthcoming. *The Making and Unmaking of the Haya Lived World.* Durham, N.C.: Duke University Press.

SIX

Nostalgia and the New Genetics

Marilyn Strathern

Let me state my problem at the outset. It is how to keep the self without being nostalgic. The nostalgia I wish to avoid is that of traditionalism; I intend nothing sentimental in the term "keep." "Sustain" might be a more apposite term, but were I to write "make" or "practice" or some such activity word, I would already have divested the self of the only way in which *it* can appear—in making, working, doing. I have always been wary of "the self" as an object of enquiry: I recognize "myself" in what I do but have the very strong sense that it is not my job, so to speak, to recognize other people's selves, since that is something only they can do for themselves.

The personal pronouns should make it clear where the self in this chapter appears.[1] It appears in a position for which I wish to argue. In having to argue for it, I also of course resist it. A position cannot be held without movement between positions, and it is this reflexive in which "I" am caught. I should add that the self in question is not to be grasped as a subject (jealous of its liberty), nor as an individual (yearning for uniqueness), nor as a person (present in others' acknowledgment), nor indeed as a predicate of discourse, though all these belong to late-twentieth-century renditions of how the self appears "to be" aware. That is because I do not wish representation on it.[2] If "the desiring, relating, actualising self is an invention of the second half of the twentieth century [a Euro-American twentieth century, that is]" (Rose 1990, xii), then its representation is already subsumed by convention. There is absolutely no point in piling on more attempts, reinventing the convention. Nikolas Rose's sequence of chapter headings has already said it: Maximising the Mind, Obliged to Be Free, Technologies of Autonomy. The last named chapter concludes with the observation: "The self that is liberated is obliged to live its life tied to the project of its own identity" (1990, 244).

For the self can only be "liberated" within a milieu of representations that would also have it otherwise. There is no end, so to speak, to the representational fix.

I want to do something else, self-consciously in a late-twentieth-century way, and make myself have an effect. Not producing the effect *of* a self, or giving evidence for it, or making "it" effective, for these would be to recreate late modern representationalism. If the effect is *of* anything, it will be of the rhetoric I use. And since in writing this introduction I already know what the conclusion will be, I can tell you at the outset that I have failed. That is, I do not think I will have accomplished the persuasion I wanted; indeed it will become clear that I arrive instead at a rhetorical impasse. One could say I succumb to my own resistance to my argument. The only comfort of course is that had I succeeded, the success of the effect would indeed have belonged to the rhetoric.

The argument is about how to sustain certain understandings of the world in a context where those understandings are written off by others as traditionalist or premodern, or, where they are not written off, are sentimentalized exactly for the same reason—in short, where they suffer too much representation. My problem is to appear neither traditionalist nor sentimental. The understandings in question concern the kind of critical response an anthropologist might want to make to current thinking about the new genetics, and in particular how to manage anthropology's relational premises. "My" problem is accordingly commuted into the problem of how to keep relationships in view without being nostalgic. It is arguing for this position that is the problem. I lay the argument out as a plot, since I had hoped some of its persuasiveness might have come from the manner of its unfolding. It will take some setting up.

THE SETUP

In considering ways in which degrees of kin have been computed in the European past, Jack Goody (1983, 134ff.) traces diverse representational maneuvers. The human body, reckoning from the head (apical ancestor) to the shoulder, elbow, down to the nails, offered one articulation of the Germanic calculus that the eleventh-century church had adopted in preference to the former Roman system. But both the computation and the means of representation were subject to dispute. He reports that canonical authors in the twelfth century followed a distinction between the "trunk" (or stem) and the "degrees." The trunk was the point of departure for reckoning degrees, but there was a dispute as to whether the point of departure should be a brother, father, or grandfather. In effect, "the trunk comprised a group of which the blood was seen as identical" (1983, 139); this could mean a set of siblings, a couple, or an individual and descendants, and each of these sets gave rise to its own system of reckoning.

Goody argues that as a property holder that stood to gain from bequests, the church had a double interest in how kinship was reckoned. It wanted to expand the range of kin prohibited from marrying (who would otherwise consolidate familial property), yet narrow the span of property heirs. The change to a Germanic computation accomplished the first, while the second motivated an emphasis away from the fraternal unity that was a feature of the Germanic system either onto the unity of the matrimonial couple, and thus onto a "direct" line of descent, or else onto the individual as a point of reference. In this last mode the trunk was assimilated to an *ipse* (self). He adds: "The visual representation of consanguinity . . . no longer consisted simply of the ordering of terms for relationships . . . but was based on an ego-oriented scheme that facilitated the computation of degrees and was in line . . . with the increasing emphasis on individuality" (1983, 142). Reinventing, in fact, a visual device already present in manuscripts then some five hundred years old, the medieval church rendered the self at once in the singular and as a node in a set of relationships.

Although dealing with historical materials, Goody writes as a social anthropologist. His particular concern is to relate such representational strategies to the interests the church then had in the devolution of property (and thus in the definition of heirs and successors), but this in turn is part of a larger comparative enterprise in which he defines European kinship by contrast first with Oriental and then with non-Eurasian systems. I draw on it as an example of anthropology's commitment to a relational view of human behavior. Relational can be taken in multiple senses: it refers to persons' interactions with other persons (the church was competing with other property holders), to the way representations work off one another (the "one flesh" of the matrimonial couple was played off against the blood bond of siblings),[3] and to the comparisons at the heart of analysis (different modes of kin reckoning). It is a commitment to a relational view that I also wish to keep for myself.

In twentieth-century anthropology this relational view is commonly concretized in the elementary concept of "relationship." I have suggested elsewhere (1992) that the study of relationships between persons (as in kin relationships) in turn keeps[4] concrete the conceptualization of relations between phenomena (whether as objects of study or as the concepts that are the means of study). In one sense relationships are infinitely extendable; in another sense relationships are also constraints. The creative possibility afforded by one mode of expression is already prefigured by its relationship to others. So any set of relations is always selective. In the same way, a commitment is always partisan.

A brief exemplification of partisanship is the order. One of the elements that has sustained my interest in feminist scholarship is its relational premise. If one cannot understand the lives of "women" without also understanding the lives of "men," and vice versa, it is also the case that one cannot understand academic feminist practice without appreciating its double relationship to liberation politics on the one hand and to critiques of modernity on the other. Yet I inevitably introduce a piece of mischief in referring to feminist issues. I know perfectly well that it is a very partial reading of feminist practice to claim a relational view for its premises. Feminist practice is equally premised on essentialist understandings:[5] womanhood is not to be understood simply in terms of conditions set up by these various relationships but is itself to be addressed as a condition. Indeed, a historically important component of feminist politics has always been the effort to *de*-relationalize women, to disown the implicit comparison, to seek descriptions not dependent on masculinist ones. Such de-relationizing was the first step toward being able to grasp "the multiple differences of condition and experience glossed and/ or derived by categorical statements concerning 'women' " (Stanley 1992, 241).

When I draw on feminist scholarship, then, I am made aware of my own partisanship. It is introduced here to make concrete the partisanship of my commitment to "a relational view," precisely because such scholarship has already made that view concrete and already embeds it in arguments from which it can never be extricated. How to make an argument concrete when everything is already concrete might be another way of rephrasing the problem I have set myself, "faithful to the insight that one never thinks in a void" perhaps. That phrase is from Rosi Braidotti's (1991, 3) rendering of certain poststructuralist thinkers who present themselves (after Gilles, Deleuze) with "questions organised around the problematisation of ideas in the 'nomadic style.' " She refers to her own dealings with the "forked formula" of (in her case) "woman and/in philosophy" as proceeding through a "carefully considered nomadism" (1991, 13). Perhaps a relational view, if not comparative anthropology itself, is already nomadic.

One might take the contrast between tradition and modernity as a similar forked formula. In introducing early European kin reckoning I wanted to give a sense of concreteness to certain present-day practices (including kin reckoning) by reference to other equally concrete renditions. At the same time these renditions are also suggestive antecedents. Yet it would be a mistake to see certain elements as traditional to European forms simply because one can find evidence of them in the past. The very contrast between the traditional and the modern is a contemporary (modernist) differentiation (cf. Robertson 1992, 152), and one can read current practices either way. An anthropologist might observe, for instance, that twentieth-century Euro-Americans who pursue their personal genealogies to find some originating location for their family are using them as their own parents or grandparents might have used them. However, it is a recent phenomenon and, given its enablement by telecommunications, high-speed transport, and commercial services that specialize in tracing family histories, perhaps a modern one as well, to turn such findings into "family gatherings." Such gatherings acknowledge what people take to be modern conditions of living—they expect to be geographically scattered through migration, occupation, or lifestyle. There is nothing traditional about getting everyone together *for such reasons*, though the endeavor echoes tradition (family gatherings at festivals or life crises) and in gathering those who are related through common ancestors the endeavor appears to be activating links that belong to the past.[6]

Perhaps it is no surprise that in contrast with other types of modern relationships, then, kinship itself may appear "traditional." Thus Anthony Giddens's open and diverse modernity is "a post-traditional order" played out against what is conceptualized as "pre-modern contexts" (1991, 189). It is "kinship ties" that offer him an example of "the prime external anchoring of the individual's life experience in most pre-modern contexts" (1991, 147; cf. Harris 1990, 53). Thus do kinship ties enter our descriptions in already concrete ways.

However, there are changes afoot, and Giddens also refers to Judith Stacey's study in California's Silicon Valley. Here "individuals are actively restructuring new forms of gender and kinship relations out of the detritus of pre-established forms of family life"—"recombinant families" (Giddens 1991, 177). The metaphorical allusion is to recombinant DNA technology or what in general parlance is known as genetic manipulation (recombinant DNA is the hybrid produced by joining pieces of DNA from different sources). But new ways of thinking about the coming together of persons made concrete in reference to contemporary genetic technology also set up the problems for the relational view that concerns me here.

I want to consider the effect of taking the new genetics literally rather than metaphorically, and in particular its effect on certain contemporary understandings of identity. I have said that my problem is the relationship of everything one knows to the parts one wants to make use of, and I suggested a parallel with my reaction to feminist practice: I know it is based on a position that at times must be taken for its essentialist virtues, yet what I want to draw from it are its relational implications. The new genetics also invites us to witness a fabrication of an essentialist understanding of human identity. In this case, however, I cannot, as in feminist debate, draw out a relational interpretation from the same body of scholarship: I can only oppose a relational view that comes from *outside* current genetic representations.

By the new genetics[7] I mean the new prominence that has been given to Euro-American knowledge about the genetic makeup of persons through the development of gene therapy (based on DNA recombinant technology) and the international human genome project (mapping the genome, that is, all the genes found in the cells of human beings). As long as genes were regarded as mechanisms whose complexity could only be guessed at, their role in explaining human affairs was relatively circumscribed. But the global mapping of the genome as a huge and complex organization now promises to rival anything Euro-Americans knew about the complexity of social or cultural life.

There are two rhetorical issues here. The first is the instant way in which that possibility has been popularly translated into the possibility of predicting not just disease patterns through a lifetime but behavioral characteristics. The director of the British Centre for Policy Studies, founded by two members of the then Conservative government,[8] was not so long ago reported as dismissing British social research ("at worst Marxist, at best stale Fabian"), instead commending his listeners to the genetic determinism of Richard Herrnstein, the Harvard author of *Crime and Human Nature*. Herrnstein was reported on the same occasion as saying that in parts of Europe 60 to 70 percent of criminal behavior was inherited, and a reporter extracted from him the admission that "there *are* different genes for different classes" (*The Independent*, May 21, 1990, original emphasis). All this is reportage, of course, though the social context in which these remarks were allegedly uttered included a representative from the British prime minister and from the Home Office, and their general import seems to have been clear. Genes offer explanations for behavior where others have failed, and policy makers are interested. Geneticists would no doubt be appalled. In explaining the current state of play in genetic technology to the public (e.g., Weatherall 1991), workers in the field are invariably careful to draw attention to interactional and environmental factors. Yet their qualifications seem to make little dent on the widespread understanding that if the genome is the entire map then eventually individual items of behavior will be traced to their individual components.[9]

But while existing arguments might well make most Euro-Americans very cautious about a genetic determinism that claims to account for social disorder, other applications of genetic knowledge have already been pressed into practice. The following month, *The Independent* (June 10, 1990) reported that a man who had pleaded guilty to having had sexual intercourse with his daughter was cleared of the charge of incest on the grounds that "he was not her father."[10] DNA testing (genetic fingerprinting) had shown he was not genetically related. Genetic fingerprinting is a technique that uses certain sequences of what otherwise appear to be "useless" bits of DNA but which have the property of being repeated many times, the pattern of repetition being unique to the individual. A person can thus be matched to his or her own cells. The current media image of a genetic fingerprint is the bar code that can be read at the checkout.

A new window seems to have been opened, then, on personal identity. It is as though what were once drawn in terms of social connections between persons can now be made present within the individual him- or herself. This leads to the second rhetorical issue.

If the first issue concerns the ease with which new understandings have been literally seized upon, and ones which privilege representation of the individual person as a bundle of individual genes, the second issue concerns the difficulty of finding new metaphors for a relational view. The need to do so is given in the kind of understandings such as those just quoted, for they set up "genetic" knowledge as bypassing "social" knowledge and, in so doing, give the individual an essentialist character.[11] Feminist politics is necessarily relational in that it exists in the necessity to make explicit the consequences of structures, institutions, and values for those whom they do not appear to privilege; if I can draw a relational view from within the praxis of feminist debate, it is because that debate is already relationally situated. With respect to the new genetics, on the other hand, I find myself *wishing to create* relationships for the knowledge it brings—to make explicit its context in human affairs; to uncover the concrete example that will show that the potential of the human genome for explaining human behavior is not self-sufficient. Even when offered new ways of visualizing the interconnectedness of all humankind[12]—and across species no less—I find myself *not* wishing to give the new genetics that rhetorical power. Hence my suspicion of the metaphor of recombinant families.

One might argue, however, that the geneticist's view of the importance of environmental factors in the development of organisms, which makes the contribution of genes something of a contingency, in affording an interactionist model also does afford a set of relational metaphors. (Lewontin [1992, 33] strikingly observes that "the external forces, what we usually think of as 'environment,' are themselves partly a consequence of the activities of the organism itself as it produces and consumes the conditions of its own existence.") Yet such a model already makes the idea of relationship concrete in one specific way. It deals with "the relationship between" an organism and its environment, and however much one sees each as the precipitate of the other, it does not provide a model for interaction between organisms in the way that models of social life deal with interactions between persons. There is a further hesitation; to find relational metaphors in these genetic representations simultaneously endorses the primacy of biological knowledge over anything else we know about the social and cultural contexts of human life. If one is to continue to give those contexts prominence, and I am committed to doing so, then perhaps relational metaphors should come from social and cultural factors themselves. That then creates its own problem: seeing such factors as "outside" the organism, and somehow secondary in turn to it, endorses current understandings of biological process as prior.

Now given that genetic endowment is (for Euro-Americans) in the first place to do with the inheritance of characteristics, and thus implies a connection between the carriers of them, it would seem that there is one area at least in which one could recover a relational view of the person: not recombinant families but kinship itself. Genes do not just provide an individual with identity, they also relate persons to one another and give them an identity as "relatives" (in English to refer to a person as a "relative" is to imply a kin relationship). Moreover, that genetic knowledge is ever only part of what constitutes people's enactment of relationships, and in that sense cannot pretend to encompass everything that is implied in being a relative. I return to the point that kinship may well have held a premier place in twentieth-century anthropological theory precisely because it is so evidently about the way people manage relationships. Surely even to begin to talk about persons related in this way will evoke a sense of social and cultural context, and thus a relational ground for genetic knowledge. However, to find a rhetorical solution in kinship also recreates the problem, as we shall see.

THE NARRATIVES

The New Genetics

Dorothy Nelkin, who writes in the fields of both social science and law, has for long been concerned with "the social power of biological information."[13] Of interest in the present context is a recent article by Nelkin and a legal colleague, Rochelle Dreyfuss, on the jurisprudence of genetics. It is a commentary on the way, the authors say, "genetics has profoundly altered the perception of personhood within our culture" (Dreyfuss and Nelkin 1992, 315). The article provides an American text that encapsulates the rhetorical issues bothering me, and I quote from it extensively (notes omitted).

> The decision to fund [the Human Genome] Initiative, the largest biology project in the history of science, at a time of significant budgetary constraints suggests its political currency. Scientists have recently developed genetic tests, familiar from the diagnostic technologies used to identify genetic abnormalities in fetuses and newborn infants, to find the markers indicating predisposition to certain single-gene disorders such as Huntington's disease. This success has bred the hope that more complex conditions, such as cancer, drug dependency, and mental illness, will ultimately be predictable and has enhanced the appeal of theories that explain human behavior in biological terms. . . . Institutions, including employers, insurers, and educators, look to biological tests to guide placement and avoid risk. Interest in genetics is also apparent in legal discourse. . . . [T]here has been a shift from essentially metaphorical uses of genetic concepts to an incorporation of biological principles into the substance of legal doctrine. . . . [G]enetic information is increasingly suggested as a tool for deciding cases in a wide variety of fields, including torts, criminal, trust and estate, family, and labor law. (1992, 313–314)

The last point can be corroborated in Britain. *The Independent* (August 12, 1992) reported DNA fingerprinting being used to substantiate a claim to a £100,000 inheritance.

Dreyfuss and Nelkin point to what they call "genetic essentialism" in the way the law is newly drawing on biology. They argue that it plays into existing cultural preconceptions about the biological basis of personhood. The importance of individual characteristics has been seen in

> psychological definitions [that] emphasize the internal developmental factors that form personality and shape identity. In western philosophy, personhood rests on the individual's ability to exercise free choice. According to Derek Parfit: "[T]o be a person, a being must be self-conscious, aware of its identity and its continued existence over time." (1992, 317)

It is this individualism that becomes overdetermined. They continue:

> Modern science provides support for defining personhood biologically, according to genetic characteristics. Geneticists are uncovering the inherited qualities that influence the course of life from childhood to old age. . . . Such tests yield only probabilistic information, for the relationship between disposition and actual expression generally remains unknown. Yet expectations about the predictive possibilities of genetic tests have created a new category of person—the presymptomatically ill, the person "at risk" . . .[14] (1992, 318)

> Society appropriates science to support prevailing values, sometimes extending it beyond the limits of well-accepted knowledge. Thus, the enthusiasm of some

members of the scientific community draws public attention to genetic relation-ships. . . . Those unable to conceive seek out surrogate mothers in order to have genetically related children. Films and articles on parent-child relation-ships suggest the importance of genetic integrity, of "flesh and blood." Geneal-ogy services are flourishing as people pursue their roots. "How to" books and articles written for adoptees stress the importance of finding one's natural or birth parents and suggest that knowing one's genetic heritage is a way to define identity. The very concept of identity is defined more in biological than in social terms. (1992, 319)

Despite the enthusiasm for genetic "relationships," the authors' concern is that the privileging of such relationships in human affairs will not be seen to lie in social practice but will be seen as a simple manifestation of "the genes" themselves. They conclude:

Observing these trends, we define a concept called "genetic essentialism." Ge-netic essentialism posits that personal traits are predictable and permanent, de-termined at conception, "hard-wired" into the human constitution. If compre-hensively known and understood these inherent qualities would largely explain past performance and could predict future behavior. (1992, 320–321)

Dreyfuss and Nelkin report, then, on what seems an emphatic cultural bias toward interpreting genetic knowledge as the source of other kinds of knowledge. The authors' point is that biological reasoning is being intro-duced into the law as literal fact when the very relationship between genetic constitution and the person as an entity with which the law must deal is in their view socially or culturally constructed. In addition, they note the specific emphasis that Euro-American culture places on the person as an individual. It is this view of the person as an individual that is doubly sustained in the idea of psychological and genetic uniqueness. In order to show the extent to which "this ideology minimizes the importance of social context" (1992, 321), they set out to show that other definitions of the person are possible. They do so in a way that dispels any fear anthropologists might have that their knowledge was of no use to anyone.

Anthropological studies demonstrate that personhood is a socially-defined con-cept. That is, the understanding of what it means to be a person and what rights are associated with personhood varies from culture to culture. . . . Examples from cultures other than our own illustrate that the social identity of an individ-ual is not a universal concept, but rather is defined by the community as part of its system of social relationships. Many societies perceive the person in terms of group identification. For example, in Bali, the use of personal names is usually avoided. More important are names that indicate relationships, such as birth order, status, and most commonly, familial relationships. Because a person is understood contextually, names will change in the course of a lifetime to reflect status in the family. A man is called by the name of his children, prefaced by "father-of," or "grandfather-of," or "great-grandfather-of." Thus, personhood in Bali is defined by social placement. (1992, 316–317)

Having established the importance of social context for the way non-Euro-Americans may understand the person, Dreyfus and Nelkin suggest that the new genetics has effected a significant transformation *within* Euro-American culture. It will influence the way the law in future handles issues that in the past have been based in what they call "community."

> Scientific and legal changes are interrelated. Both the cultural beliefs that shape science and the knowledge that emerges from science are readily incorporated into legal doctrine. Thus, the transformation of "personhood" into an essentially genetic concept has important consequences for legal thought. If personal identity is no longer understood in relational terms, then doctrines dealing with community—relationships among people—must be reconsidered. Because genetic essentialism is a deterministic concept, it negates assumptions about free will, thereby putting into question much of the law concerning responsibility, intent, condemnation, and punishment. (1992, 321)

But wait a moment. "If personal identity is *no longer* understood in relational terms . . ." No longer? Looking back over their argument one realizes that they use the anthropological material to introduce a double universal where the anthropologists might want to claim only one. As they said, anthropology demonstrates that personhood is a socially defined concept, that is, it is part of the human condition to live as social beings, and that includes having ideas about other human beings, personhood being just such an idea. In the particular forms they take, we recognize such ideas as cultural creations. We can indeed take this as a universal. But this is then conflated with a second claim that also appears in their argument as a universal.

Dreyfuss and Nelkin use the Bali example to present a particular image of personhood. The example turns on the importance *to the Balinese* of the contextualization of the person in social relationships, and on how they visualize this. Balinese do to kinship through names what Euro-Americans do through (say) genealogical trees: the changing name makes concrete a perception of the social nexus in which persons live. However, although Dreyfuss and Nelkin are carefully specific (they actually contrast "cultures that perceive the person in relational terms [e.g., Bali]" with "those that emphasize the importance of the individual" [1992, 317]), the rhetorical place that the Balinese hold in their account suggests otherwise. It is as though this particular (Balinese) image of personhood illustrated a fundamental universal truth about all manifestations of personhood.[15] In fact, as the authors are also aware, Balinese are being as rhetorical in this image of personhood as they are in the way they wish to make relationships visible (in their case, through the system of names; cf. Cohen 1990).

Now one could say that when Balinese define persons contextually, they are making relations socially visible, whereas when Euro-Americans define persons as individuals through biological criteria they conceal the social context in which relations are sustained, although in the second case "social context" would either have to be shown as ideologically present but subordinate or else as an analytic construct on the observer's part. Conversely one could say that Balinese in turn conceal the individuality of persons, or that the Bali counterpart to Euro-American individualism is not individualism at all but is the unique "position" that social placement creates for each person. Yet none of this would imply that some kind of generic or universal view of personal identity in relational terms is being superseded by the new genetic essentialism.

However, suppose that Dreyfuss and Nelkin are merely being rhetorical about the fact that in Euro-American culture one can certainly witness such a displacement. They would then be reporting on a simple historical sequence, and indeed that is what they elsewhere imply. The law that once rested on a double base of both individual and what they call community values is being invited to emphasize one at the expense of the other. And they draw on Euro-American ideas of *kinship* to show where a relational understanding of personal identity once existed, pointing specifically to the institution of the family as a setting for community values.

Forget patriarchy for a moment and read this:

> When the family was regarded as the primary setting for care, education, and emotional support, stability was one of the law's central goals; familial relationships were rarely disturbed. Divorce was difficult. Courts often resolved paternity disputes using devices such as [estoppel rules]. . . . These estoppel rules [16] . . . may have originated in a non-technological society's search for a method to determine the fact of paternity. But they also preserved the status quo. By assuring children continued contact with the significant persons of their lives, these rules evidenced the high value placed on social relationships. (1992, 321–322)

Then they go on to draw the parallel:

> When the person is reconceptualized as a genetic entity and forging genetic relationships becomes a goal, legal protection for these social interests weakens. For example, *Johnson v. Calvert*, a case the [American] press described as "genetics vs. environment," was a dispute over the custody of a child conceived through *in vitro* fertilization (IVF). The Calverts donated their gametes (egg and sperm) to create a so-called test tube baby. Because the wife could not

sustain a pregnancy, the couple hired Johnson to carry the fertilized embryo to term in her womb. The dispute began after Johnson refused to relinquish the child, Christopher, at his birth. When genetic tests revealed a high probability that the Calverts were Christopher's biological parents, the court awarded them sole custody. . . . Thus the court defined the child as a genetic entity—a packet of genes—on the assumption that shared genes are the crucial basis of human relationships.

Genetic essentialism has also affected other parental relationships. Thus, legal protection generally is not accorded to the tie between a child born to a lesbian mother and her non-gestational partner no matter how long the relationship between the two parties has endured. (1992, 323–324 passim)

Their examples move from cases where we might consider relationships well bypassed (not all relationships seem worth upholding simply because they are evidence of "the relational"), to those where the bypassing of relationships seems, as they want us to see, an injustice. Despite that equivocation I accept their principal point, that insofar as genetic essentialism is given such an emphasis in people's explanations of human affairs, it is important to focus attention on the issues this emphasis neglects: the relational understanding of persons and personal identity.

Yet to find such an understanding in kinship recreates the problem for me. And that is because of the way kinship is being made concrete: the appeal is to tradition. Any political move to rescue a relational view *from the past* surely becomes its own undertaker. Anything one might want to say about the contemporary relevance of Euro-American family relationships is already compromised by presenting its roots in previous times, never mind among the Balinese. It seems all too nostalgic. Do not master narratives rather easily include opposition to themselves as nostalgia, that is, as already internalized and captured alternatives? (The words are Kathryn Sutherland's, personal communication). As a potential master narrative the new genetics needs no tradition to back it up, and most emphatically it is not yet a subject for the nostalgia industry. Rather, it is (about) our technological future, and thus speaks rhetorically of immediate concerns.

Nostalgia

Here I must state a desire.[17] I would like to be convinced by Dreyfuss and Nelkin; I welcome their use of anthropology; I sympathize with their cause and appreciate the remarkable set of issues they have opened up for discussion. I am also apprehensive about appearing to detract from their clear and important message. It is the rhetoric, not the message, that is at issue. I believe their defense of a relational view also gives reasons for others to ignore it. For in the context of arguments about genetic innovation, culture itself, and thus the force of the argument about cultural variability, seems lost in the sense of loss it conveys. Roland Robertson (1992, 159) cites Frederic Jameson on the point: culture, he says, "is a 'privileged area in which to witness' the current appetite for images of the past."[18] Here is the rhetorical place the Balinese seem to hold in Dreyfuss and Nelkin's account: they illustrate what no longer seems true for us. Let me examine this form of nostalgia.

Robertson catalogues the various senses of loss which previous forms of nostalgia have articulated, as well as offering a critique of what he calls the kind of modern synthetic nostalgia (after T. Nairn) built into the origins of sociology, and its acceleration in late-twentieth-century evocations of the past. The result is seen in nostalgic theories about the present. He suggests that contemporary society is in a new phase of globalization that is generating a "diffuse kind of wilful, synthetic nostalgia amounting to something like the global institutionalisation of the nostalgic attitude. All the more reason," he adds, "to eliminate nostalgia from social theory as analysis and thematize it as an object of sociological analysis" (1992, 158). It is, he says, a theory of nostalgia that we need. Nostalgia not only carries negative overtone, it has lost a kind of innocence. To point out that something is nostalgic draws attention to its deliberate evasion of the present.

This last phrase (after Hutcheon) comes from Debbora Battaglia's (n.d.) consideration of nostalgia in the lives of late-twentieth-century Trobriand Islanders. It prompts me to adapt Robertson's injunction about shifting from means of analysis to object of enquiry; perhaps (to paraphrase) one can eliminate nostalgia from cultural theory and thematize it as an object of cultural analysis.

Battaglia makes it clear that in one sense there is no way that, as a Euro-American, I can be nostalgic about the kind of past that makes Trobriand Islanders nostalgic. Indeed, in considering how islanders living in the capital of Papua New Guinea deal with their reenactments of the past, she finds herself describing *another kind* of nostalgia, and one that seemingly lies outside the history to which Robertson refers. This enables me to turn nostalgia into a forked formula. If "culture" can be mobilized to convey a sense of loss, "cultural analysis" suggests that the one thing we have not lost is a sense of nostalgia. Now the Euro-American nostalgia that Robertson calls synthetic is nostalgia for past conceptual systems, for cherished values, for kinds of behavior, that is, *for* "tradition" or *for* "culture." But Euro-Americans also have nostalgia for persons and places and land. While we might imagine that we could share other people's nostalgia for a vanishing culture, we cannot share it for the particular persons they miss or the places they have left. Here your (their) nostalgia is most emphatically not my (our) nostalgia. This is the sense in which Trobriand elaborations are distinctive.

If I evoke Trobrianders, it is not for them to be "my Balinese." On the contrary it is to make concrete a simple distinction between a nostalgia for past customs and practices and a nostalgia for (say) persons and places. These mobilize different ways of embodying the past in the present. The point is exemplified in Richard Werbner's (1991, 109) recent account of Kalanga living in Zimbabwe. Personal narratives given by elders from a single family divide into two genres (though he refers only to the first as "nostalgia"). Although both narratives of the past deal with people and events, he suggests that the one is cast in terms of an irreversible break between past and present, when the narrator looks back to good times where conditions of life were qualitatively different, while the other is a catalogue of cautionary recollections about how the significance of people's acts carry forward in time, when the circumstantial details about disputes and inheritance are forewarnings for present relationships. With respect to the first, insofar as Euro-Americans regard themselves as custodians of (the self-appointed representers of) world history or world culture, then for me as a Euro-American the narrator's loss is also my loss. With respect to the second, however, I can only draw an analogy between the details of the narrator's life and my own and am relieved I do not have to worry over the same things. In short, there is a different rhetorical effect to these genres.

Synthetic nostalgia mourns for what is missing from the present, and thus creates representations *of* the past as the place where what is gone was once present. Dreyfuss and Nelkin mourn the fact that relational views of the person—and the legal framework of the community they associate with these views—were once present in "the family." Trobrianders in Port Moresby may similarly speak wistfully, in synthetic vein, of being displaced in time and space. At the same time, when they evoke the past, it is also to evoke the social context of relationships "at home," and these relationships have a substantive effect on the living, present capacity of Trobrianders to act in town. An example would be the kinds of feelings aroused by planting the highly prized yam in urban soil in order to enact relationships that at home depended on the place (among other things) where the yams were planted. It is not just that feelings are aroused, but that they must be aroused. The planting is only efficacious if the planter can imbue it with his own attachment to the act and thus by recalling relationships already in place (see further, Battaglia 1992). Such nostalgia as accompanies the Trobriand recall of an origin is a way of making explicit the fact of origin, an attachment to a past that is and can only be realized in the present. The origin of the act does not, as it were, exist till the act is done.

In their own evocations of the past, Battaglia makes evident, Euro-Americans may avoid the sentimentality of synthetic nostalgia by irony, that is, by awareness of the contrariness of imagining a "real" distance between past and present. The idea of tradition encapsulates the view that one can relive what one is already separated from. Family gatherings can be carried off with irony in this way. However, these Trobriand reenactments do not need irony; she calls them "nostalgic practice." In these contexts, the past is the substance of (present) relationships: it is, so to speak, being acted out now. And I want to borrow this second notion of nostalgia, not in order to make Trobriand culture relevant to a Euro-American one, but in order to grasp a rhetorical possibility that the practice of their substantive enactments offer. Let me refine Dreyfuss and Nelkin's appeal to kinship. Let me imagine a "kinship" for contemporary Euro-American practices that deals with the past as tradition but where the past is at the same time more than tradition. I imagine it not only with synthetic but also with substantive nostalgia.

Synthetic nostalgia would come from thinking that the relational view of personal identity is *best exhibited* in the past. That is, that past configurations of family relations provided not just examples but exemplars of a relational view, and ones that have since been transformed by modernity. As a consequence, the past is taken as a real preexisting entity by virtue of its break from the present. Only if one keeps the break in mind can one overcome nostalgia with irony. At the same time, it becomes vaguely phoney to "recreate" the past in the present, to think of bringing back large families or the significance of relationships. However positively one may regard the values in question, to take values for their traditional status assigns them to tradition. We can rejoice or regret, but what is always reinforced is the passing of tradition. So the past itself acquires its presence, in this mode, by being the subject of representation.

Substantive nostalgia would come from thinking that kinship is the constitution of the past in the present, the enacting of obligations because a *prior relationship* exists, belonging to a family because of one's name, being a child because one's parents had children. Kinship exists in these ties. There is no possibility of an ironic break here because the presence of the past is not affected by whether or not one represents it. Insofar as it displays its own effect, and thus needs no representation, then one might add that there is no break with one's origins and no distance to mediate. Evidence of its being practiced lies in the relationships themselves.

It is probably difficult for Euro-Americans to talk of the second type of nostalgia without recalling the first, for their late-twentieth-century discourse of innovation and technology that is heavy with the newness of the present (Campbell 1992) continually asserts the breaks with the past that recreates all nostalgia as synthetic nostalgia. To evoke family, kinship, and relationships is often to be nostalgic in this sense. Nonetheless, one could perhaps make out a case for substantive nostalgia—the always-present effect of relationships, the necessary contemporaneity of working through the origins of one's obligations and feelings—and thus a case for the significance of a relational view not as part of a traditional but as part of a modern world. (Since one would wish to collapse the distinction between tradition and modernity, technically one would have to speak of a postmodern world.) A relational view would consequently appear *not* as the trait of some epoch or culture, which can always be written off, but as a pointer to the inevitable relationships in which individual persons are enmeshed. And here Dreyfuss and Nelkin's choice was surely right—here kinship surely comes into its own as a concrete and contemporary mode for visualizing the substantive effect of prior relations.

Thus one could argue that the anthropologist has to take Euro-American kinship constructs as significantly as he or she takes them anywhere. They do not belong to 'tradition' except insofar as they are represented as such. Rather, they contribute to the making of persons in the present world, including those who have to live the impossible politics of the enterprise culture (Heelas and Morris 1992). But making kinship constructs constitutive of the present in this particular manner presents *me* with the most taxing problem of all. It is, of course, one of my own making.

THE STING

The problem is this. Were I to translate the American anxieties that have been so well voiced into ones to which I can respond from the vantage point of English kinship, I would be forced to acknowledge that English kinship was never only about relating. If only it were otherwise! If only I could take refuge in the simple idea that kinship only attends to relationships, I could then draw on the workings of kin relationships as an internal cultural critique on genetic essentialism—shorn of all breaks with the past, naturally, and with thoroughly contemporary import. But I am done in by my own reflections on English constructs, and doubly insofar as I take them as an exemplar of Euro-Americanism. English kinship constructs, it seems to me, are as much about reproducing the essentialism of individuality as they are about relational definitions of personal identity. That is precisely their contemporary power.

The evidence is already there in the Dreyfuss and Nelkin article when the authors refer to the biological view of personhood. Where does that come from but Euro-American ideas about procreation, the uniqueness of flesh and blood ties, the significance of nurturing persons to the point of their leaving home and being able to do without parents, and so forth? In fact, one could go back over their text and reread all their evidence for genetic essentialism as evidence of Euro-American kinship thinking. For example, it is not a desire for genes that makes a person seek surrogacy, but a desire to be a parent by having a child of one's own. The genetic connection is instantiated as a kin relationship, and if it is instantiated as a relationship, what is simultaneously instantiated is the uniqueness of the individual child. This uniqueness may be seen from one of two perspectives. Uniqueness may be attributed to the child's placement in a circle of relatives (cf. Edwards et al. 1993); here the individual is the outcome of relationships. But from the very possibility of being able to "see" these relationships "in" the individual person also come Strathern's three facts of English kinship: the individuality of persons, the diversity of characteristics, and the individual's ability to reproduce individuals (1992, 14, 22, 53). These facts belong to a thoroughly modern epoch.

Such kinship constructs offer their own forked formula. Indeed in retrospect (that is, with present preoccupations in mind) one might look back at those medieval computations of degree of relatedness: when the "self" (*ipse*) was put at the heart of schemes of reckoning, the same genealogy yielded both the tracing of relationships and the centring of the individual as a point of reference. A similar duplex is present in the recent debates to which Dreyfuss and Nelkin give voice. *Both* sides of the debate are recreated within the very material (kin relationships) they (and I) would like to enlist, in a much more partisan way, on one side alone. Indeed this is where we find culture, in the constant re-creation of the reasons for our problems, in the holographic distribution (Oyama 1985, 114; cf. Wagner 1991) of motifs over a field.

One cannot then go to one bit of culture (kin relationships) to rescue us from other bits (genetic essentialism). What one can perhaps do is expose partisanship as such. Genetic essentialism is as real a part and culturally as much a part of Euro-American thinking as is the value Euro-Americans put on relationships and a relational view.[19] When it leads to bigotry, new forms of racism, intolerance,and the threat of a "genetic underclass" (Nelkin 1992,

190), it cannot be disowned as cultural fact; it can be disowned as thoroughly one-sided, narrow-minded, and prejudiced, in short as partisan.

An anthropology that evades the individualism built into Euro-American kinship constructs simply commits synthetic nostalgia. Yet in pointing to this individualism, I am at the same time locating the (cultural) origins of the significance currently attached to genetic essentialism. I am practicing substantive nostalgia. Indeed, we may turn it around the other way and say that modern understandings of genetics afford a powerful idiom for making the Trobriand practice of substantive nostalgia concrete for us. Euro-American ideas about genetic influence imagine a literal embodiment of genetic information whose original is unknown *till the moment it takes effect* in the manifestation of some characteristic or other. That is, what was laid down in the past exists in the effect it has in the present. I am short-sighted because, among other things, of the genes my ancestors carried, and thereby I make those genes evident and manifest their contemporary presence. At least, that is my understanding of the way genetics was always pressed into the service of kinship thinking.

Like Dreyfuss and Nelkin, I have borrowed from a non–Euro-American culture, although in my case not a visualization of a relational view of the person but a visualization of a kind of nostalgia. Like them I did so in order to contrast a culturally prevalent miasma with a different state of affairs. Unlike them I have a rhetorical end in view which does not wish to make my preferred mode a traditional one, that is, claim a kind of shared past. On the one hand, I want to avoid synthetic nostalgia for bygone cultures. Substantive nostalgia, on the other hand, seems attractive insofar as it is about the making of a particular present. Yet this other fork lands me in a similar impasse. For substantive nostalgia leads me to apprehend exactly how past ideas about the biological base to English kinship (to choose among Euro-American exemplars) endure, like so many forewarnings, in the present fascination with genetics.

However, the new genetics is the sting in the tail of the sting. Its applications are imagined in a highly anticipatory mode; its creation of the presymptomatically ill, its eagerness to prevent characteristics appearing before they can do harm, its concern with what will happen before anything is made present, all give a new edge to Dreyfuss and Nelkin's critique of genetic essentialism. It is as though selves could be erased before they appear. That is, it is as though they could be worked on (the potential characteristics carried by genes) before one knows how to interpret their effects. The very relationship between "the gene" and everything that leads it to have a material presence becomes notionally bypassable, most notably in ideas attributed to single-gene diagnosis but generally in the kinds of therapies imagined for the future. One might turn after all, then, to an older genetics to find a relational imagery encapsulated there, not in order to resurrect the restricted idea of "a relationship" between organism and environment but to resurrect *the interpretive effort* that goes into the explanation of manifest characteristics. The geneticist's interactionist paradigm implied that genes never exhibited *themselves*.[20] Insofar as they are mediated by (the form of) their manifestation they are also mediated by persons in the analytical effort required to assess their effect. It is such effort that reminds us of the partisanship of all interpretations; it also makes evident the relational matrix of the effect persons have on one another.

Yet much popular rhetoric would see no interpretive mediation necessary—genes are imagined as the messages themselves.[21] Which returns me to my rhetorical problem: how to keep relationships in view without being nostalgic. I have offered an interpretation of nostalgia that substitutes appeal to the past with acknowledgment of the present, but that solves not at all how to keep relationships in view. It is no comfort that only a relational view of cultural process could yield the insight that kinship is connected to other aspects of Euro-American culture, and that only a relational view enables one to specify the power that essentialist imagery has on the late-twentieth-century imagining of "real" personal identity. From where do I find the metaphors to make that relational view as concrete to apprehend as the new genetics itself?

NOTES

1. My thanks to Debbora Battaglia for allowing me to cite from her unpublished paper and for the provocation it produced, to Sarah Franklin for conversations on the new genetics, to Kathryn Sutherland for her observations, and to Nigel Rapport for taking "the self" seriously. Most of the examples cited in this chapter came to my attention via the good offices of colleagues; I am most grateful to Sarah Franklin (Braidotti), Frances Price (*Independent,* June 1990), David Shapiro (Lewontin; Nelkin and Dreyfuss), Margaret Stacey (*Independent,* May 1990). Members of the Women in Philosophy Group who met in Cambridge, the Department of English at Manchester University, and the Faculty of Social Science at the Open University have commented on drafts of this chapter to my profit, as has Peter Fitzpatrick.

2. Perhaps akin to the Whalsayman's protest, so eloquently rendered perplexing by Cohen (1990, 4), that he had "a right" to "be himself." (Cohen's distinction between form and meaning is in turn akin to the difference I deploy between representation and effect.)

3. The depiction of personal genealogies followed the attempt to depict degrees of relatedness. Euro-American genealogies are today commonly imagined as family trees, with apical ancestors at the top, and the spreading branches of numerous descendants below. However humble the social origins of one's ancestors, to be able to trace the identity of a remote ancestor brings a sense of superiority, the sheer numbers of persons whom one can name as family members being in itself a source of pride. The genealogy invites people to visualize these relationships in certain ways: they calibrate time with rank with trees. It was once a moot question whether time should be represented as flowing up or flowing down, a question itself posed by having to represent flow on a two-dimensional surface that was hung or looked at from a fixed position and thus had a top and a bottom. The solution might seem obvious: ancestors are those from whom descendants "descend" and therefore suitably at the top (of the page, the genealogical tree). Yet introducing the image of the tree that equated time with growth introduced other possibilities. After all, a tree appears to grow from its roots: so ancestors who are prior to their descendants are really the family roots, and indeed some early genealogies depicted them at the bottom. Yet that is also an illusion, since the branches and the root system of a tree grow simultaneously outward from a center; perhaps the ancestors should be the core or trunk of the tree.

4. "Keep," with a nod to Durkheim and Mauss (1963 [1903]). The antecedents are long here. Tully (1980, 10) points out that Locke stressed the role of social relations in natural law theory. In his 1662 *Essay on the Law of Nature* Locke wrote that "most precepts of this law [of nature] have regard to the various relations between men and are founded on those."

5. Essentialist with respect to *the means of understanding* shared specificities in women's condition, not with respect to the nature of "women." ("Feminism is not merely a 'perspective' or a viewpoint on the world, not even as epistemology or a theory of knowledge about it; feminism constitutes an *ontology*, a different way of being in the world which is noted in the facts of oppression" [Stanley 1992, 253; original emphasis].)

6. English kin-keepers (after Firth et al. 1969) may be regarded as gathering in the family on the basis of their knowledge of past ties. As one woman observed of her mother's sister who had played such a role: "She was a touch with the past" (Edwards 1993, 52).

7. As Emily Martin (1990) uses the term (I appreciate the permission to cite this unpublished paper).

8. Lord Joseph and Margaret Thatcher.

9. Rabinow (1990) sees the dual process of individualisation and totalisation which Michel Foucault pointed to as characteristic of modern systems of knowledge-power in the way in which new social and political entities (genetic populations) can be created by observed variations of genetic frequencies, yet in being so created will appear not to be created by social and political criteria.

10. "It is only in light of scientific advances that it has come to light that the appellant is not the father of the girl concerned," said the Advocate Depute (*The Independent*, June 10, 1990).

11. I am not as pessimistic as Miringoff (1991), who seems to regard social under-

standings as hard-won and the impetus toward social and community values in the United States as fragile. I should add here that there is nothing inherently essentialist in the concept of the individual. On the contrary there is a long tradition in Western/ Euro-American thought that takes the individual subject as constituted in its responsiveness to others. Relatedness creates the uniqueness of the individual (and see common English expressions of this in Edwards et al. 1993). The *rhetorical problem* is that to focus on "the individual" often appears to extract it from such fields.

12. I have already quoted (e.g., Strathern 1993) the vision offered by the embryologist Grobstein who insists on the genome as the common property of humankind and the relatedness of the species thereupon. "It is this commonness that is our collective heritage and property as human beings. And it is about possible changes in this collective property . . . [that] all human beings have the right to be consulted" (Grobstein 1990, 20).

13. The title of her book with Laurence Tancredi (1989; see also Nelkin 1992). And in the context of scientific accountability, see Price 1990, 124.

14. The person who has no symptoms but is "known" to carry a genetic disorder.

15. My own rhetoric is evident here, since I blow this up out of all proportion in the account that follows. (Elsewhere Dreyfuss and Nelkin bring one back to the "sharp contrast" between "relational definitions of personhood" and [Euro-American] ideas that minimize the importance of social context.

16. "[S]uch as Lord Manfield's rule, which estopped a husband from denying that he fathered the children born to his wife during his marriage, or equitable estoppel, which prevented a mother from denying the fatherhood of a man whom she had permitted to nurture her child" (Dreyfuss and Nelkin 1992, 321–322).

17. Like Crapanzano's (1992) luckless messenger who in conveying what other persons desire thinks he (Hermes) must make them relate to the message he conveys.

18. I am cheating here. The "culture" that is the subject of the remark is the culture of "cultural studies," dominated by the media's traffic in images. However, it is not so removed from some Euro-American understandings about the detachability of "culture" from the "real world." During the course of a project reported on elsewhere (Edwards et al. 1993), I recall speaking to a moral philosopher who has been long engaged with issues in embryo research and to a historian of science and technology who has long reflected on biotechnology's place in society. Both were bemused at my insistence on the significance of cultural ideas. Their responses were almost the same. People always have them, don't they? They will always come up with their own versions of the world, won't they? One cultural idea is as good as another, isn't it?

19. Thus Nelkin and Tancredi (1989, 160) correctly observe that there are "cultural conditions [that] legitimate . . . the tendency toward biological reductionism in explaining social or behavioral problems."

20. What is exhibited is their effect, even when the effect is other "genes" ("Not only is DNA incapable of making copies of itself, aided or unaided, but it is incapable of 'making' anything else . . . the proteins of the cell are made by other proteins, and without that protein-forming machinery *nothing* can be made" [Lewontin 1992, 32; original emphasis]).

21. See Oyama's (1985) critique; further reflections are to be found in a companion essay, "Surrogates and Substitutes" (Strathern 1993).

REFERENCES

Battaglia, Debbora. n.d. "Whose Irony Is This? Trobriand Dialogues in the National Press." Manuscript. Stanford University, Department of Anthropology.
———. 1992. "Displacing Culture: A Joke of Significance in Urban Papua New Guinea." *New Literary History* 23:1003–1017.
Braidotti, Rosi. 1991. *Patterns of Dissonance: A Study of Women in Contemporary Philosophy*. Oxford: Polity Press.
Campbell, Colin. 1992. "The Desire for the New: Its Nature and Social Location as Presented in Theories of Fashion and Modern Consumerism." In *Consuming Technologies: Media and Information in Domestic Spaces*, edited by R. Silverstone and E. Hirsch, 48–64. London: Routledge.
Cohen, Anthony P. 1990. "Rites of Identity, Rights of the Self." Inaugural Lecture, Edinburgh University, November 22.
Crapanzano, Vincent. 1992. *Hermes' Dilemma and Hamlet's Desire: On the Epistemology of Interpretation*. Cambridge: Harvard University Press.
Dreyfuss, R. C., and D. Nelkin. 1992. "The Jurisprudence of Genetics." *Vanderbilt Law Review* 45:313–348.
Durkheim, Emile, and Marcel Mauss. 1963 [1903]. *Primitive Classification*. Translated by R. Needham. London: Cohen and West.
Edwards, Jeanette. 1993. "Explicit Connections: Ethnographic Enquiry in Northwest England." In *Technologies of Procreation: Kinship in the Age of Assisted Conception*, J. Edwards, S. Franklin, E. Hirsch, F. Price, and M. Strathern, 42–66. Manchester: Manchester University Press.
Edwards, Jeanette, Sarah Franklin, Eric Hirsch, Frances Price, and Marilyn Strathern. 1993. *Technologies of Procreation: Kinship in the Age of Assisted Conception*. Manchester: Manchester University Press.
Firth, Raymond, Jane Hubert, and Anthony Forge. 1969. *Families and Their Relatives: Kinship in a Middle-class Sector of London*. London: Routledge and Kegan Paul.
Giddens, Anthony. 1991. *Modernity and Self-Identity: Self and Society in the Late Modern Age*. Oxford: Polity Press.
Goody, Jack. 1983. *The Development of the Family and Marriage in Europe*. Cambridge: Cambridge University Press.
Grobstein, Clifford. 1990. "Genetic Manipulation and Experimentation." In *Philosophical Ethics in Reproductive Medicine*, edited by D. R. Bromham, M. E. Dalton, and J. C. Jackson, 15–30. Manchester: Manchester University Press.
Harris, C. C. 1990. *Kinship*. Milton Keynes: Open University Press.
Heelas, Paul, and Paul Morris. 1992. *The Values of the Enterprise Culture: The Moral Debate*. London: Routledge.
Lewontin, R. C. 1992. "The Dream of the Human Genome" [review article]. *New York Review of Books*, May 28, pp. 31–40.
Martin, Emily. 1990. "Biopolitics: The Anthropology of the New Genetics and Immunology." Paper presented at the American Anthropological Association meeting, New Orleans.
Miringoff, Marque-Luisa. 1991. *The Social Costs of Genetic Welfare*. New Brunswick, N.J.: Rutgers University Press.

Nelkin, Dorothy. 1992. "The Social Power of Genetic Information." In *The Code of Codes: Scientific and Social Issues in the Human Genome Project,* edited by D. K. Kevles and L. Hood, 177–190. Cambridge: Harvard University Press.

Nelkin, Dorothy, and Laurence Tancredi. 1989. *Dangerous Diagnostics: The Social Power of Biological Information.* New York: Basic Books.

Oyama, Susan. 1985. *The Ontogeny of Information: Developmental Systems and Evolution.* Cambridge: Cambridge University Press.

Price, Frances V. 1990. "The Management of Uncertainty in Obstetric Practice: Ultrasonography, In Vitro Fertilisation, and Embryo Transfer." In *The New Reproductive Technologies,* edited by M. McNeil, I. Varcoe, and S. Yearley, 123–153. London: Macmillan.

Rabinow, Paul. 1990. "Galton's Regret." Paper presented at the American Anthropological Association meeting, New Orleans.

Robertson, Roland. 1992. *Globalization: Social Theory and Global Culture.* London: Sage.

Rose, Nikolas. 1990. *Governing the Soul: The Shaping of the Private Self.* London: Routledge.

Stanley, Liz. 1992. *The Auto/Biographical I: The Theory and Practice of Feminist Auto/Biography.* Manchester: Manchester University Press.

Strathern, Marilyn. 1992. *After Nature: English Kinship in the Late Twentieth Century.* Cambridge: Cambridge University Press.

———. 1993. "Regulation, Substitution and Possibility." In *Technologies of Procreation: Kinship in the Age of Assisted Contraception,* J. Edwards, S. Franklin, E. Hirsch, F. Price, and M. Strathern, 132–161. Manchester: Manchester University Press.

Tully, James. 1980. *A Discourse on Property: John Locke and His Adversaries.* Cambridge: Cambridge University Press.

Wagner, Roy. 1991. "The Fractal Person." In *Big Men and Great Men: The Personification of Power in Melanesia,* edited by M. Godelier and M. Strathern, 159–173. Cambridge: Cambridge University Press.

Weatherall, David. 1991. "Manipulating Human Nature." *Science and Public Affairs* [The Royal Society; BAAS]:25–31.

Werbner, Richard. 1991. *Tears of the Dead: The Social Biography of an African Family.* International African Institute. London: Edinburgh University Press.

SEVEN

Production Values: Indigenous Media and the Rhetoric of Self-Determination

Faye Ginsburg

This chapter addresses the recent development of video, film, and television made by, with, and for Aboriginal Australians.[1] I will sketch, briefly, the context for the emergence of Aboriginal media as it has been shaped by the interdependence of specific local situations and historically changing government policies, as well as transformations in consciousness of Aboriginal and Euro-Australians, and in the broader transnational polity known as the fourth world. Of particular interest in the context of this volume is how differing notions of selfhood are negotiated through such work: these range from notions of community authorship embedded in indigenous understandings of cultural property and expression, to concepts of self-determination that have emerged in the political struggles of Aboriginal people in relation to the Australian state, to notions of individual self-expression valorized in venues for media exhibition in which indigenous media work is shown to (mostly) non-Aboriginal audiences. Although my analysis of these discursive intersections is somewhat preliminary, it can help clarify the complex intersections of the multiple rhetorics of self-making that shape the lives of contemporary indigenous peoples, rhetorics that undergird state media policies as well as the transnational circulation of indigenous imagery.

The ever-increasing involvement of Australian Aboriginal people in visual media production over the last two decades[2] is part of the legacy of the Labor government's liberal left policy toward Aboriginal "self-determination" from 1972 through 1975 (Leigh 1988). Since then, the range of televisual media generated with and by Aboriginal Australians corresponds not only to differences in the experiences of those living in urban, rural, and traditional settings, but also to the diverse social positions Aboriginal people occupy, the various ways they have attempted to gain visibility and cultural control over their own images, and the manner in which they are differentially positioned in Australia's "national imaginary" (Hamilton 1990). Unfortunately, this diversity has not always been accounted for by those setting broadcast policy (Molnar 1989, 147),[3] despite a broader ideological climate favoring multicultural expression as an acceptable version of the Australian polity (Hamilton 1990).[4] While a policy of administered self-determination for Aborigines (with all its contradictions) was put in place over the last decade, in practice, Aboriginal culture is flattened, reified, and assumed to be homogeneous.

Aboriginal work in film and video is as diverse as the Aboriginal producers who make it, from traditional bush-living people to urban dwellers whose history of contact with Euro-Australian culture may go back as far as two hundred years. Urban Aboriginal film- and videomakers, such as avant-garde filmmaker/photographer Tracey Moffat, are comfortable in claiming individual authorship of works, operating comfortably within the structures of an international independent film world, albeit addressing problematic issues of Aboriginal identity (Langton 1993, 13; Murray 1990).[5]

At the other end of the spectrum are traditional people living in remote areas of central, northern, and western Australia, whose contact history may be as brief as a few decades, yet who have been experimenting with video production strategies to suit their very local concerns for over ten years. As Aboriginal anthropologist and cultural activist Marcia Langton describes it: "Much of the production in remote Australia is the work of community groups [that] . . . have their own production values, distinct aesthetics, and cultural concerns" (1993, 14). I address here (for the most part) work being produced by these remote, relatively traditional groups, video work that is understood to be authored by the community (or segments of it) rather than by individuals, and whose audiences are primarily but not exclusively themselves.

SITUATING INDIGENOUS MEDIA

My work is part of an ongoing effort to open a "discursive space" for indigenous media that respects and understands the work on its own terms. Langton has identified such efforts as necessary "to develop a body of knowledge on representation of Aboriginal people and their concerns in art, film, television, and other media and a critical perspective to do with aesthetics and politics, drawing from Aboriginal world views, from Western traditions and from history" (1993, 28). New discursive possibilities have emerged in anthropology and cultural studies that self-consciously reject notions of "authenticity" and "pure culture" (Appadurai and Breckenridge 1988b; Hall 1992). In line with such theories of cultural production, indigenous media can be understood as part of a powerful new process in the construction of contemporary and future indigenous identities (Ginsburg 1991; T. Turner 1992).[6] Taking my lead from ideas expressed by Aboriginal media makers, I have argued elsewhere that indigenous productions are often directed to the mediation of ruptures of time and social relations in ways that point to a cultural future (Ginsburg 1991). They address history by bridging relations between generations when the activities of "traditional culture" are no longer effective in doing so. This may be very direct, for example by stimulating ceremonial production in a new generation, as occurred with the Nambiquara in Brazil who reinstituted a nose-piercing initiation as a result of watching themselves on video (Carelli 1988).

Video works also provide an especially important arena for Aboriginal self-production. As a novel form, new media enable a re-visioning of social relations with the encompassing society which more traditional indigenous forms cannot so easily accommodate. In this way, indigenous media have been used as vehicles for reproducing and transforming cultural identity for indigenous people who have experienced massive political, geographic, and economic disruption (Carelli 1988; Michaels 1987a; T. Turner 1992). Thus, tapes are often imaginative Aboriginal interpretations of not only powerful relationships to land, cosmology, and ritual but also fragmented histories of contact with Europeans; continued threats to language, health, culture, and social life; and positive efforts to deal with such problems in the present. In media production, Aboriginal skills at constituting both individual and collective identities through narrative and ceremonial performance are engaged in innovative ways that are simultaneously indigenous and intercultural.

While new media forms have been embraced by many members of indigenous groups as powerful means of collective self-production that can have a culturally revitalizing effect (Ginsburg 1991; T. Turner 1990), this should not mask the fact that the introduction of these forms has also been experienced as a threat. The broad marketing of VCRs and the launching of communications satellites also brought the hegemonic shadow of mainstream television into the daily lives of indigenous people living in remote areas. The impact has been especially powerful for traditional Aboriginal people in the Central Australian desert since the 1980s, for whom satellites and VCRs catalyzed their first efforts at media production, based on both local initiatives and state interventions.

ABORIGINAL MEDIA

In the Australian context, "television" refers to the use of electronic broadcast technologies for the production and dissemination of images to large or small groups of people via television monitors. Practically speaking, this encompasses a range of practices. Perhaps the most interesting are those that use combinations of low-format video and televisual technologies but whose organization and work are uniquely embedded in local Aboriginal communities, for example, the Warlpiri Media Association (WMA) at Yuendumu or EVTV at the Pitjantjatjara settlement of Ernabella in South Australia. These local groups have explicitly challenged the imposition of mainstream Australian television by making and showing their own and other Aboriginal videotaped productions. These might include everything from extensive taping of ceremonies, to local sports events, to MTV-inspired music videos performed with Aboriginal bands singing in native languages.

By contrast, the Aboriginal commercial television broadcaster, Imparja, delivers programming very similar to that viewed by American television consumers, except for one or two evenings a week when programs by and about Aboriginal Australians can be seen. One lineup might segue from a situation comedy, to regional news, to indigenously produced segments on Aboriginal bush methods for cooking kangaroos, to an international soccer match. The broader cultural meanings of such unexpected combinations that emerge in Imparja's televisual "flow" are a constant source of discussion. One need only turn on a television in Central Australia to provoke a lively debate as to whether Aboriginal programs are a mere token presence in the commercial context or the opening wedge for transformations in the ways that Australians are envisioning their own diversity.

Thus, in Australia, Aboriginal media have become a visible element in what Annette Hamilton calls the Australian "national imaginary," part of a social formation that operates by the conflation of rhetorics and implicit ideologies of individual and national selfhood (Hamilton 1990).[7] Drawing on ideas from Benedict Anderson, Edward Said, and Jacques Lacan, Hamilton uses the term to describe the means by which contemporary nation states constitute "imagined communities" through the circulation of televisual images even more than the print media discussed by Anderson in his now classic work (Anderson 1983). Hamilton uses Lacan's idea of the Imaginary (as the mirror phase in human development when the child sees its own reflection as an "other") to describe imaginary relations at the collective level. Mediated encounters with those who are culturally different can be seen as ourselves looking at ourselves while we think we are seeing others, for example, in films

such as *Crocodile Dundee* in which the outback and Aboriginal knowledge
play a critical role in validating the settler presence in the country (Hamilton
1990, 18).

Such representations of the Australian nation circulate in an increasingly
"internationalised image-environment" (1990) in which representations of
indigenous peoples now carry a heavy load, as Donna Haraway (1992) has
pointed out so cogently. Aboriginal media have become implicated in these
commodified images of Aboriginality, which now include "hi-tech primitives." Such imagery escapes the control of indigenous makers as it romanti-
cizes them, for example, in Wim Wenders's short-lived 1992 film *Until the
End of the World*, in which a crew of Aboriginal technicians assist mad scientist Max Von Sydow in his efforts to use technology to make visible people's
dreams, thus playing quite literally on the notion of Dreamtime, the English
gloss for Aboriginal cosmological systems. This is in contrast to those images
of natives presented in traditional settings (the noble but exoticized savage)
or as victims (the vanishing race) that are increasingly problematic for Euro-
Australian (and other) consumers who are aware of and uncomfortable with
our implication in the lives and historical circumstances of these "Others."
Conversely, I would argue, there is a pleasure for such consumers in regarding the image of the indigenous videographer as a kind of bush cosmopolitan,
at ease with both tradition and Western advanced technology; such an image
evokes a kind of futuristic nostalgia, even if it masks inequality and culpa-
bility.

Commodified images of Aboriginal producers along with Aboriginal
acrylic paintings and popular music groups such as Yothu Yindi are part of
the cultural capital on which contemporary Australia builds its national image
for consumption and circulation in the arenas of tourism, political affairs,
and the marketing of culture overseas (Beckett 1988; Hamilton 1990; Myers
1991). As a relatively benign example, the Australian consulate circulated a
festival of Aboriginal film and video in the United States in 1993 as part of
the United Nations Year of Indigenous Peoples.

Still, although their perspectives certainly differ, indigenous producers,
sympathetic media activists, and government administrators alike see both
the activity and product of Aboriginal cultural production in film and video
(and other forms) as linking diverse populations as well as the past, present,
and future in various "imagined community/ies" of the nation.[8] In service
to that vision, the capabilities of Aboriginal media to transcend boundaries
of time, space, and even language are seen as effectively mediating historically
produced social ruptures. Thus, support for Aboriginal media comes in part
from the imagined role they can play in constructing an inclusive if uneasy

vision of the nation that, at least televisually, is beginning to take account of its Aboriginal citizens.

OUTBACK TELEVISION

Prior to the setting of government policy, two important community-based Aboriginal media associations developed at the relatively traditional remote communities of Yuendumu on Warlpiri lands on the edge of the Tanami Desert in Central Australia, northwest of Alice Springs; and Ernabella on Pitjantjatjara lands in South Australia, just south of Uluru (Ayers Rock). Both are Aboriginal settlements with highly mobile populations that can vary from five hundred to a thousand over the course of a year. Founded by missionaries in the 1940s, they became self-governing by the 1970s and retain infrastructures consisting of a community store, a town office, a police station, a primary school, a health clinic, a church, an art association, and local broadcast facilities. Langton succinctly describes the Warlpiri settlement of Yuendumu:

> On the surface, Yuendumu is a desolate "fourth world" settlement of concrete block "houses," windswept red soil, minimal employment, poor diet and health. But there is a strong determination by the Warlpiri people to survive, to fight back, to retain a heritage of great antiquity and continuity. (1993, 59)

In 1982, American researcher Eric Michaels, a consultant for the (then) Institute of Aboriginal Studies, went to Yuendumu to conduct a long-term study of the impact of media on traditional Aboriginal people in Central Australia. Michaels had been trained in the United States by Sol Worth, whose famous project of teaching filmmaking to Navajo suggested the possibility of culturally distinct practices of media production and reception (Worth and Adair 1972), an empirical argument against McLuhan's view that the medium is the message (McLuhan 1966).

While Yuendumu and many other Aboriginal communities had not received the steady flow of mainstream Australian broadcast television available in most non-Aboriginal communities, they were acquainted with popular cinema through community viewings of rented films, attending theaters in the nearby town of Alice Springs, and the circulation and viewing of videos on their own or resident whites' VCRs. By 1983, essentially every extended family had access to at least one VCR (9 for 900) on which they could view rented tapes in "appropriate groupings respecting avoidance restrictions and other traditional constraints on congregating" (Michaels 1986, 8). Michaels's research on Aboriginal media reception drew heavily on Nancy Munn's insightful work on Warlpiri iconography (Munn 1973), suggesting analogies between their experiences of production and reception of video and their production and reception of their traditional graphic system. "For Warlpiri viewers," according to Michaels,

> Hollywood videos . . . are very partial accounts which require a good deal of interpretive activity on the part of viewers to supply contents as well as contexts which make these stories meaningful. When home video made it possible for Warlpiri to control the place and membership of viewing groups, it became possible to assemble the small interpretive communities which are associated with other performances in which stories are told and their associated graphics displayed. At this point, video viewing became a most popular and persuasive camp activity. (1986, 12)

Following Worth's model, Michaels helped train people to produce their own videos based on Aboriginal concerns. The Warlpiri Media Association (WMA) grew out of this activity. Between 1982 and 1986, Warlpiri videomakers produced hundreds of hours of tapes on subjects ranging from traditional dances, to a piece memorializing a massacre of Warlpiri people by whites, to recording of local sports events. Originally, the tapes were circulated via camp VCRs. In April 1985, WMA established its own very local low-power TV station via a homemade transmitter that provided a way to broadcast locally produced tapes to the community and to pull in the signal for the state television channel, the Australian Broadcasting Corporation (ABC). WMA and other similar operations were considered illegal because the state had no licensing category for such small-scale broadcasters (Michaels 1986). This bureaucratic vacuum for Aboriginal media was an important index of the ambivalent governmental stance toward Aboriginal initiatives.

From the local perspective, government neglect had positive effects. It meant that there was room for community control and the development of an innovative production style, both aesthetically and in work relations, appropriate to local social organization, narrative conventions, and communicative strategies. For example, the substance and formal qualities of the tapes have a distinctly Warlpiri sensibility. In contrast to the free-floating signifiers that characterize most Western televisual semiotics, Warlpiri tapes show an intense focus on particular landscapes, consistent with the way traditional Aboriginal knowledge is made meaningful by associations with specific geographic locations (Michaels 1986). But of equal if not more importance is the social organization of media production; the ways in which tapes are made, shown, and used reflect Warlpiri understandings of kinship, group responsibilities for ceremonial production, and the control of traditional knowledge (Michaels 1986). Traditional Aboriginal production does not em-

phasize the creative "self-expression" of individuals or assign them responsibility as authors. All cultural production is part of a broader effort at self-
production in the collective sense.

> Stories are always true, and invention even when it requires an individual agent
> to "dream" or "receive" a text, remains social in a complex and important sense
> that assures truth. Rights to receive, know, perform, or teach a story (through
> dance, song, narrative, and graphic design) are determined by any identified
> individual's structural position and social/ritual history within an elaborately
> reckoned system of kin. Novelty can only enter this system as a social, not an
> individual invention. Not only is one's right to invent ultimately constrained, it
> is particularly constrained with respect to the kinship role for it is the geneaol-
> ogy of an item—not its individual creation—which authorises it. (Michaels
> 1987b, 65)

Similar developments occurred at Ernabella, a remote Pitjantjatjara community in South Australia (Batty 1993; Molnar 1989, 25ff.; N. Turner
1990). There, in 1983, local people, with the help of white schoolteachers,
began producing video programs that immediately became quite popular. By
April 1985, Ernabella Video Television (EVTV) was established, providing
"local broadcasting on the world's cheapest community television transmission system (less than $1,000 worth of equipment purchased from a 10 cent
surcharge on cool drinks in the store)" (quoted in Dutchak 1992, 48). In
seven years, EVTV has produced thousands of hours of community television. Broadcast is strictly regulated by the local media committee, made up
of male and female elders, in terms of both substance—so that images are
not shown that violate cultural rules regulating what can be seen (e.g., sacred
ceremonies)—and timing, so that television does not interfere with social
activities.

Locally based groups like WMA and EVTV are able to maintain Aboriginal
control over video production and viewing in keeping with their own community standards. As Philip Batty, a media activist in Central Australia, as-
sesses it, WMA and EVTV "had managed to establish their own local television service funded through their own local resources and became familiar
with the basic processes of television production, long before the arrival of
television via satellite" (1993, 114). This was accomplished by funding and
managing their projects on their own terms and applying an active if basic
knowledge of television technology in locally relevant and meaningful ways,
which gave them the confidence and community consciousness to deal with
the arrival of mainstream television via satellite when that occurred. Addition-
ally, video production in remote communities has had a remarkable effect in
terms of cultural production. For example, for Pitjantjatjara people, the work

of EVTV "had the effect of engendering a kind of local renaissance in traditional dance, performance and singing. The various video programmes depicting the actual land where the dreaming lines were located gave renewed
strength to traditional beliefs and values within the communities" (Batty
1993, 113).

SATELLITES AND AIR RIGHTS: IMPARJA

Over the 1980s, the Australian government took an increasing interest in the
development of Aboriginal media. The problematic nature of state intervention is exemplified in Imparja, Australia's first Aboriginally owned commercial television station. The story of Imparja originates in concern over the
consequences for Aboriginal people of the launch of Australia's first communications satellite, AUSSAT. This event brought the destructive potential of
broadcasting commercial television to remote areas of the nation for the first
time, including many Aboriginal settlements and communities in Central
Australia whose geographic isolation had protected them from such intru-
sions. After much debate regarding what was the appropriate action to take,
members of CAAMA, the Central Australian Aboriginal Media Association,
who had organized a very successful and indigenously based radio station,
mobilized and made a bid for the satellite downlink license to Central Australia. Their petition to the Australian Broadcasting Tribunal was made initially
as a symbolic assertion of the presence and concerns of that region's Aboriginal people. Much to their surprise, their proposal was taken seriously. As it
turned out, the national Tribunal provided the arena for the articulation of
state media policies that, at least nominally, were in support of the concerns
of remote-living Aboriginal people.

In 1986, after considerable struggle with more commercially viable competitors, CAAMA won the license. The private commercial station they now
own, Imparja, began broadcasting in January 1988, serving approximately
one hundred thousand viewers in Central Australia, over 25 percent of them
Aboriginal, as opposed to 2 percent in the general population (Batty 1993).
Thus far, in addition to public service announcements and logos with images
of Aboriginal people, Imparja has been regularly broadcasting programs produced by CAAMA. Their most successful program is *Nganampa—Anwer-
nekenhe* ("Ours"), a magazine show on Aboriginal culture produced in four
Aboriginal languages (with English subtitles), broadcast on Thursday nights.
In its first two years, Imparja was viewed with great optimism, although some
media activists prophesied that Aboriginal interests would be swallowed up
by the "survival needs" of a costly commercial television operation. For ex-

ample, in the opinion of Michaels, government support for self-determination was based largely on Western economic and cultural models that attempt
to construct an Aboriginality that is a mirror of Euro-Australian culture: "the
emphasis on technology and high production values (intended rather than
realised) seems part of a more general attempt to constitute Aborigines as
'world Class, export quality' natives. They feature what the government sees
to be 'good' Aborigines doing productive (i.e., non-Aboriginal) things"
(1986, 63). Many since have come to agree with the pessimists; they are
disappointed by the lack of Aboriginal presence in Imparja's programming
and personnel, arguing that two to three hours out of seventy hours a week,
even at prime time, is insufficient Aboriginal programming. Freda Glynn, an
Aboriginal woman who was cofounder and Director of CAAMA (from 1980
to 1991), resigned because of internal disagreements over the way Imparja
was developing.

> Our original aim was to get some control over the satellite so that we could use
> it to suit our own purposes. . . . I remember saying that television was like the
> second invasion of our country, that it would be just as destructive as alcohol.
> . . . We wanted to see a lot of black faces, people speaking our local languages.
> . . . We were especially interested in using it for educational purposes. . . .
> Maybe this can still happen . . . but look at Imparja now, it's no different to
> any other commercial TV station. . . . In a way, it has become what we tried to
> stop. (Glynn, quoted in Batty 1993, 123).

In contrast to small-scale groups like WMA and EVTV, Imparja is a large
multimillion-dollar station in which information flows follow the imperatives
of commercial television oriented toward mass audiences. The so-called need
for advertising—and therefore programs that are assumed to draw big audiences—supersedes investment in programming for Aboriginal viewers, in
keeping with the management's orientation toward profits and Euro-Australian interests. To the white management, Aboriginal programming is regarded as not lucrative because there is a drop-off in European viewers; advertisers do not view Aboriginal people as significant consumers. And this
does not even begin to address the complexities of mass broadcasting from
an Aboriginal perspective. For example, how are images of people who have
died to be handled, when Aboriginal mortuary rituals prohibit the circulation
of names or images of those who have passed away?

Nonetheless, Imparja, as one of the first indigenously owned commercial
television stations in the world, is held up by the government as a successful
example of Aboriginal development and self-determination, a ploy that sometimes backfires (Batty 1993, 18). The comments of a 1991 Nigerian visitor
to Imparja (cited in Batty 1993) are instructive:

He had been told that this was the only Aboriginal-owned television station in Australia, and was therefore keen to see how an indigenous group ran such a service and in what ways it differed from mainstream stations. He was amazed to learn that the federal government had given the local Aboriginal people more than $18 million to set up and run Imparja over three years, but perplexed to discover that the station only employed four Aboriginal people out of a total staff of thirty-two and that Imparja's programming was 98% white! While Imparja is totally cloaked in the rhetoric of "Aboriginal self-determination" and is supported by many millions of "Aboriginal dollars" provided by the government, the main beneficiaries do not appear to be Aboriginal. (1993, 122)

The case of Imparja makes clear that even well-intentioned attempts to increase the visibility of Aboriginal accomplishments and concerns in the mass media are often fraught with complexities that white policy makers would rather ignore. In an international climate characterized by a problematic rhetoric of "self-determination," state officials are in the contradictory position of creating government programs promoting indigenous self-expression, yet wanting to claim that Aboriginal initiatives are evolving through a (collective) self-initiated process (Beckett 1988; Rowse 1992). Even more ironic, the mastery of new communication forms as a means of resistance and assertion of rights is often motivated by dire political circumstances created by the very governments that also provide much of the necessary support for production, a telling instance of a system some have labeled as "welfare colonialism" (Beckett 1988).[9] Thus, rhetorics of self-determination can gloss the fact that the scale and "rules" of mass media may be completely inappropriate to traditional Aboriginal concerns and efforts to use media as a site for self-production and cultural reinvention.

LOCAL KNOWLEDGE VERSUS THE GLOBAL VILLAGE: THE TANAMI NETWORK

As my last example, I want to discuss the recent development of the Tanami Network. In this case, state-of-the-art video technology is being used in the service of reviving Aboriginal communication patterns in which local areas are the center from which information emanates, a reversal of the European model that sees the urban cities as the center and the remote communities as the periphery.

When I was in Australia in 1988, criticisms of Imparja by more remote Aboriginal media associations had escalated. Regarding Imparja as deaf to their complaints, people at Yuendumu became engaged in an effort to develop communications in ways more suited to their concerns and activities. Along with three other Aboriginal communities in the Tanami area of Central Australia (Lajamanu, Willowra, and Kintore), they formed the Tanami Network, a video conferencing system that uses satellite signals to link these settlements to one another and to the urban centers of Alice Springs, Darwin, and Sydney. The compressed video technology allows groups of people to see and hear one another via what some have called a "space-age picture telephone" (O'Loughlin 1992). As an indication of their interest, the communities jointly contributed over $350,000 in mining royalties and other community funds to establish this system.

Their sentiments were articulated at a workshop at Yuendumu in 1990 when the technology was first demonstrated to the community. There, two paintings by a Warlpiri woman, Jeannie Nungarrayi Egan, were used to show different models of communication. In the first painting, depicting the current hegemonic model, Warlpiri communities are shown as dependent for information on *kardiya* (white people's) centers such as Alice Springs or Darwin. The second painting represents the Tanami Network's decentralized, interactive model, in which large white settlements are not privileged over smaller Aboriginal ones.

When I was at Yuendumu in 1992, shortly after the network had been put in place, Peter Toyne, a former principal of the Yuendumu school who has been active in organizing the network, placed its goals in cultural and historical context from a Warlpiri perspective.

> The establishment of the Tanami communities over the last 50 years severely disrupted the traditional network of information and personal contacts which existed amongst people in the area. The Aboriginal people have responded by attempting to reassemble the earlier network through the use of motor vehicles . . . outstations . . . and through such telephone and radio links as have escaped the restrictive control of non-Aboriginals in the communities. . . . Aboriginal community members have stated repeatedly that they want the links to work out family things and help keep the traditions and Aboriginal law strong. . . . The Tanami Network is being developed in the belief that it offers a completely new line of approach to many of these problems by changing the basic dialogue through which the services are planned and delivered. (Toyne 1992, 1)

The Network has already been used for purposes as diverse as "sorry business" (funeral arrangements), driver's education, and long-distance marketing of Aboriginal art to places such as Santa Monica (Toyne 1992). While some are skeptical of the expense and specialized nature of the technology at a time when so many basic needs—health, nutrition, shelter—are not adequately served, others are intrigued by the Tanami Network's possibilities, using arguments like those articulated by Eric Michaels: "Producing Aboriginal community media in locales with no productive economic base . . . could prove more successful than agricultural, industrial, or other material development projects, precisely because of the traditional interest and expertise in information management" (1987b, 69).

For Euro-Australian policy makers, their interests in this new project are enmeshed in their construction of Aboriginality in the current "Australian imaginary," Australia's media-savvy natives as a mirror of an ideal Euro-Australian middle class: clever and up-to-date, yet conservative. A headline in Australia's capital—"Resourceful Aborigines use latest technology to preserve tribal life" (*Canberra Times*, March 20, 1992)—captures one dimension of this construction. For policy makers, the Tanami Network offers a positive affirmation of initiative on the part of remote-living Aborigines. Thus, whatever its final outcome or relative utility, one can see in the Tanami experiment an ironic convergence of Aboriginal interests in self-production via the use of televisual technologies to reconstitute regional connections, and national rhetorics of indigenous self-determination.

TRANSNATIONAL MEDIATIONS

Indigenous media producers not only inhabit national public cultures but are also part of "global cultural flows" (Appadurai and Breckenridge 1988a, 1). As Aboriginal people become more knowledgeable about media production and representation, they can provide alternatives to the internationally popular but distorted imagery of the technologically able but traditionally exotic indigene, as in the Wenders film. In contrast to such commodified representations, Aboriginal media producers are also engaged in arenas constitutive of an emergent global fourth-world/first-nations identity[10] in which different rhetorics of self are summoned in support of indigenous media.

One can see how these different rhetorical structures come to bear in events organized for the exhibition of indigenous media production. Most prominently, in exhibition venues organized by and for indigenous people, media is framed by a rhetoric of self-determination not in the economic entrepreneurial sense of the Australian state but in a way that evokes nationhood and political independence while implicitly suggesting the privileging of collective interests over those of the individual. Yet in Aboriginal venues associated with the showcasing of independent film and video, indigenous work is drawn into Western rhetorics of self-expression that valorize the individual as a political or artistic agent. Implicit in this rhetoric is a person detached or even in opposition to a broader polity. Recent shows of indigenous film/video organized by dominant cultural institutions situate them as new forms of aesthetic/political production, focusing on "individual makers" in places associated with "auteurship" in the arts, such as the New Museum (1990), the Museum of Modern Art (1990, 1993), or the Walter Reade Theater at Lincoln Center (1992), all sites of exhibition of indigenous media. Although this has been changing as the broader zeitgeist in the West embraces multicultural and identity-based politics as frames for the exhibition of various expressive media, the structures for showing work in most cases still put forward "the artist," repressing the embeddedness of individual artistic production in broader social and political processes.

This is in contrast to the views of indigenous media producers who almost never speak of themselves as artists concerned primarily with aesthetics and formal issues, detached from communal concerns. Rather than accepting the dominant culture's model of the media text as the expression of an individuated self, they stress the *activities* of the production and reception of indigenous media as processes of collective self-making, part of a continuum of social action for Aboriginal empowerment. This position is especially evident in the rhetoric used at international film/video festivals for the work of indigenous peoples, which have burgeoned since 1985. For many, these festivals are preferred venues, over more "high culture" national institutions that privilege the notion of autonomous individuals whose needs for expressive activity override other concerns. These events are becoming the basis for constituting an emergent organization of indigenous media producers, such as the First Nations Film and Video Makers World Alliance formed at the September 1992 Dreamspeakers Festival in Edmonton, Canada, or the Native American Producer's Alliance formed at the Deadwood Festival in January 1993.

The social relations built out of these media practices are helping to develop support and sensibilities for indigenous actions for self-determination, locally, nationally, and internationally. Self-representation in media is seen as a crucial part of this process (Langton 1993). As an example of how these goals are being put into action, Dreamspeakers has already spun off into a First Nation's Film Festival held in Sydney in July 1993, organized by Aboriginal documentary maker Frances Peters, in which 50 percent of the works are Aboriginal and the rest are from other indigenous groups. Clearly, the transnational social relations built out of media practices are creating new arenas of cooperation that transcend local and even national borders.

In conclusion, I want to suggest that indigenous media has been able to flourish in part because of the social and discursive spaces created by the disjunctures and mutual misapprehensions in the multiple rhetorics of self-making that shape the funding, production, and reception of such work in

both dominant and Aboriginal cultures, as well as in transnational circuits.
However misguided, government policies built on strictly economic models
of self-determination have helped mobilize support for this work as a productive activity, often harnessing funding to bureaucratic agendas such as tapes
on using health care or social security systems. Interestingly, even work
funded for the most utilitarian of purposes on the part of the state often is
reconceived in creative ways that tie contemporary problems to the horrific
effects of the colonial encounter, a narrative refusal of a victim status that is
to be "solved" by state aid. Aboriginal producers see their media work, whatever its topic, as enabling them to assert their own cultural and historical
realities to themselves and the broader societies that have stereotyped or rendered them invisible.

Exemplary of a different disjuncture in the rhetorics of self-making is the
problem of exhibiting indigenous work in institutions built on rhetorics of
individual self-expression that characterize discussions of expressive media in
Western cultures. By contrast, indigenous media works often have a form of
communal authorship embedded in complex claims of rights to tell and re-
ceive cultural knowledge, positions that complicate structures of distribution
and public culture in which the (media) artists' position is valued as being
outside or critical of society. Instead, indigenous producers situate their work
as continuous with struggles for political self-determination. In the imaginative space of film, video, and television lie possibilities for Aboriginal communities to envision their current realities and possible futures, and to find new
arenas for collective self-production and self-representation that create links
among indigenous makers around the globe.

NOTES

1. Parts of this chapter appeared in an earlier work entitled "Aboriginal Media and
the Australian Imaginary," published in the Spring 1993 issue of *Public Culture*. For
research support, I am grateful to the Research Challenge Fund of New York University (1988) and the John Simon Guggenheim Foundation (1991–1992). This piece
could not have been written without the help of Fred Myers and Francoise Dussart
in 1992 concerning the logistics and languages of Aboriginal research in the field and
out. I am grateful to Philip Batty, Annette Hamilton, Freda Glynn, Francis Jupurrurla
Kelly, Ned Lander, Marcia Langton, Mary Laughren, Michael Leigh, Judith and David MacDougall, Michael Niblett, Tim Rowse, and Peter Toyne for their insights and
assistance.

2. Different aspects of this involvement are summarized nicely in essays by film
historian Michael Leigh (1988), filmmaker David MacDougall (1987), as well as the
late Eric Michaels (1986) and communications scholar Helen Molnar (1989)—who

reminds us that many remote-living Aborigines have been producing their own radio programming since the 1970s, "leaping over the print generation to begin recording their languages, stories, music and culture" (Molnar 1989, 148).

3. While to Euro-Australians, different "traditional" groups may seem undistinguishable, linguistic variation alone makes it clear that they are not a monolithic block; of the two hundred Aboriginal languages originally spoken, approximately sixty are still in active use today (Black 1983, 3).

4. There was no effort to establish Aboriginal broadcast policy until the early 1980s, when questions were raised about the potential negative consequences of the 1985 launch of a communications satellite, AUSSAT, on remote-living Aboriginal people (Wilmott 1984).

5. For anthropological analyses of Aboriginal "self-determination" and the production of Aboriginal identity in relation to the state, see Beckett 1988.

6. The term "indigenous media" respects the understandings of those Aboriginal producers who identify themselves as "First Nations" and indexes the political circumstances they share with other indigenous people around the globe. Whatever their cultural differences, these groups all struggle against a legacy of disenfranchisement of their lands, societies, and cultures by colonizing European societies, as occurred in Australia, the United States, Canada, and most of Latin America. "Media"—whether referring to satellites or VCRs—evokes the huge institutions of the television and film industries that tend to overwhelm the local cultural specificities of small-scale societies, while privileging commercial interests that demand large audiences as a measure of success. While the institutional dimensions of media—especially television—shadow their intersection with the lives of indigenous people, they do not determine the outcome. For that reason, I also stress another meaning of media: the activity of mediation.

7. For a similar articulation of this idea, also see Dermody and Jacka 1988.

8. For example, this was evident in an Alice Springs newspaper article announcing the recent debut of an Aboriginal compressed video network in Australia's Central desert: "Tribal business has gone space age in the outback" (O'Loughlin 1992).

9. The Department of Aboriginal Affairs began funding Aboriginal broadcasting initiatives in 1980. Since 1984, it has provided more than $1 million each financial year to support regional Aboriginal broadcasting (Department of Aboriginal Affairs 1989).

10. Some of these festivals include the Native American Film Festival, held regularly in San Francisco and New York City; the Two Rivers Festival held in Minnesota in the fall; the Pincher Creek World Festival of Aboriginal Motion Pictures, which has been replaced by Dreamspeakers, convened in September 1992 in Alberta, Canada; and the Interamerican Film Festival of Indigenous Peoples, held every two years in South America.

REFERENCES

Anderson, Benedict. 1983. *Imagined Communities*. London: Verso.

Appadurai, Arjun, and Carol Breckenridge. 1988a. "Editor's Comments." *Public Culture* 1(1):1–4.

―――. 1988b. "Why Public Culture?" *Public Culture* 1(1):5–9.

Batty, Philip. 1993. "Singing the Electric: Aboriginal Television in Australia." In *Channels of Resistance,* edited by T. Downmunt. London: British Film Institute.

Beckett, Jeremy, ed. 1988. "Aborigines and the State in Australia." *Social Analysis, Special Issue Series,* no. 24 (December).

Black, P. 1983. *Aboriginal Languages of the Northern Territory.* Darwin: Darwin Community College, School of Linguistics.

Carelli, Vincent. 1988. "Video in the Villages: Utilization of Videotapes as an Instrument of Ethnic Affirmation among Brazilian Indian Groups." *Commission on Visual Anthropology Newsletter,* May, pp. 10–15.

Department of Aboriginal Affairs. 1989. *Aboriginal Australia: Broadcasting.* Canberra: Government Publishing Service.

Dermody, Susan, and Liz Jacka. 1988. *The Screening of Australia: Anatomy of a Film Industry.* Sydney: Currency Press.

Dutchak, Philip. 1992. "Black Screens." *Cinema Papers* 87 (March–April):48–52.

Ginsburg, Faye. 1991. "Indigenous Media: Faustian Contract or Global Village?" *Cultural Anthropology* 6(1):92–112.

Hall, Stuart. 1992. "Cultural Studies and Its Theoretical Legacies." In *Cultural Studies,* edited by L. Grossberg, C. Nelson, and P. Treichler, 277–294. New York: Routledge.

Hamilton, Annette. 1990. "Fear and Desire: Aborigines, Asians, and the National Imaginary." *Australian Cultural History* 9:14–35.

Haraway, Donna. 1992. "The Promises of Monsters: A Regenerative Politics for Inappropriate/d Others." In *Cultural Studies,* edited by L. Grossberg, C. Nelson, and P. Treichler, 295–337. New York: Routledge.

Lacan, Jacques. 1982. *Ecrits: A Selection.* Translated by Alan Sheridan. New York: Norton.

Langton, Marcia. 1993. *Well, I Saw It on the Television and I Heard It on the Radio.* Sydney: Australian Film Commission.

Leigh, Michael. 1988. "Curiouser and Curiouser." In *Back of Beyond: Discovering Australian Film and Television,* edited by Scott Murray, 70–89. Sydney: Australian Film Commission.

MacDougall, David. 1987. "Media Friend or Media Foe?" *Visual Anthropology* 1(1):54–58.

McGregor, Alexander. 1988. "Black and White Television." *Rolling Stone,* no. 415:35ff.

McLuhan, Marshall. 1966. *Understanding Media.* New York: Dutton.

Michaels, Eric. 1986. "Hollywood Iconography: A Warlpiri Reading." Paper presented at the International Television Studies conference, British Film Institute, London.

―――. 1987a. *For a Cultural Future: Francis Jupurrurla Makes TV at Yuendumu.* Melbourne: Art and Criticism Monograph Series.

―――. 1987b. "Aboriginal Content: Who's Got It—Who Needs It?" *Art and Text* 23(4):58–79.

―――. 1988. "Bad Aboriginal Art." *Art and Text* 28 (March–May):59–73.

Molnar, Helen. 1989. "Aboriginal Broadcasting in Australia: Challenges and Promises." Paper presented at the International Communication Association conference, March.

Munn, Nancy. 1973. *Warlbiri Iconography.* Ithaca, N.Y.: Cornell University Press.

Murray, Scott. 1990. "Tracey Moffatt." *Cinema Papers* 79:19–22.

Myers, Fred. 1991. "Representing Culture: The Production of Discourse(s) for Aboriginal Acrylic Painting." *Cultural Anthropology* 6(1):26–62.

O'Loughlin, Genny. 1992. "Tribal Business Has Gone Space Age in the Outback." *The Advocate,* p. 2.

Rowse, Tim. 1992. *Remote Possibilities: The Aboriginal Domain and the Administrative Imagination.* Darwin: Australian National University, Northern Aboriginal Research Unit.

Said, Edward. 1978. *Orientalism.* London: Pantheon.

Toyne, Peter. 1992. "The Tanami Network." Presented to Service Delivery and Communications in the 1990s conference, Darwin.

Turner, Neil. 1990. "Pitchat and Beyond." *Artlink* 10(1–2):43–45.

Turner, Terence. 1990. "Visual Media, Cultural Politics, and Anthropological Practice: Some Implications of Recent Uses of Film and Video among the Kayapo of Brazil." *Commission on Visual Anthropology Review* (Spring):8–13.

———. 1992. Defiant Images: The Kayapo Appropriation of Video. *Anthropology Today* 8(6):5–15.

Wilmott, Eric. 1984. *Out of the Silent Land.* Canberra: Government Printing Office.

Worth, Sol, and John Adair. 1972. *Through Navajo Eyes.* Bloomington: Indiana University Press.

CONTRIBUTORS

Debbora Battaglia is associate professor of anthropology at Mount Holyoke College, writing generally on the aesthetics of productive social action. Her work focuses on subject-object relations across cultures, with an emphasis on Melanesian personhood and social memory and forgetting. Among her publications is *On the Bones of the Serpent: Person, Memory and Mortality in Sabarl Island Society* (University of Chicago Press, 1990), and she is currently working on *The Self Displaced: Essays on Themes of Urban Trobriand Identity.* She also writes on self aesthetics and new bio-technologies.

Daniel Boyarin is Taubman Professor of Rabbinic Culture in the Department of Near Eastern Studies at the University of California at Berkeley. In addition to numerous articles that have appeared in journals such as *Diacritics, Critical Inquiry,* and *Representations,* he has written *Intertextuality and the Reading of Midrash* (Indiana University Press, 1990), *Carnal Israel: Reading Sex in Talmudic Culture* (University of California Press, 1993), and *A Radical Jew: Paul and the Politics of Identity* (University of California Press, 1994).

Jonathan Boyarin's work in Jewish cultural studies focuses on the dynamics of Jewish community in the twentieth century, the relations between Jews and their various Others, the politics of memory, and rhetorics of space and time. The books he has written and edited include *From a Ruined Garden: The Memorial Books of Polish Jewry* (with Jack Kugelmass; Schocken Books, 1985), *Polish Jews in Paris: The Ethnography of Memory* (Indiana University Press, 1991), *Storm from Paradise: The Politics of Jewish Memory* (University of Minnesota Press, 1992), *The Ethnography of Reading* (University of California Press, 1993), *A Storyteller's Worlds: The Education of Shlomo Noble in Europe and America* (Holmes and Meier, 1993), and *Space, Time, and the Politics of Memory* (University of Minnesota Press, 1994). He lives on the Lower East Side in New York City with Elissa Sampson, Jonah, and Yeshaya.

Faye Ginsburg is associate professor of anthropology at New York University, where she is Director of the Graduate Program in Culture and Media and Director of the Rockefeller Center for Media, Culture, and History. Much of her work focuses on the lives of activists engaged in social transformation. She is the author of *Contested Lives: The Abortion Debate in an American Community* (University of California Press, 1989) and is currently working on *Mediating Culture,* a book about indigenous media makers in Australia.

George E. Marcus is professor and Chair of the Department of Anthropology at Rice University. His chapter in this volume derives from his long-term interest in upper classes in decline and transformation. He is the author of *Lives in Trust: The Fortunes of Dynastic Families in Late Twentieth-Century America* (with Peter Dobkin Hall; Westview Press, 1992), and editor of the Chicago University Press's "Late Editions, Cultural Studies for the End of the Century," an annual series of books that probe contemporary change through conversations, interviews, and biographical profiles. The first book in this series is *Perilous States: Conversations on Culture, Politics, and Nation* (1994).

Marilyn Strathern is William Wyse Professor of Social Anthropology at the University of Cambridge. Problems in the anthropology of gender relations have preoccupied her since her first fieldwork in Papua New Guinea. Otherwise her interests are divided between Melanesian (*Women in Between: Female Roles in a Male World,* Academic Press, 1972) and British (*Kinship at the Core: An Anthropology of Elmdon,* Cambridge University Press, 1981) ethnography. Her *The Gender of the Gift: Problems with Women and Problems with Society in Melanesia* (University of California Press, 1988) is a critique of anthropological theories of society and gender relations as they have been applied to Melanesia, while *After Nature: English Kinship in the Late Twentieth Century* (Cambridge University Press, 1992) comments on the cultural revolution at home and *Partial Connections* (Rowman and Littlefield, 1991) is a monograph on comparative method.

Roy Wagner is professor of anthropology at the University of Virginia. Much of his work deals with the ethnology of Melanesian peoples, especially in the areas of myth and conceptual synthesis. His contribution to this volume updates and considerably refigures the critiques of American lifestyles initially presented in his *The Invention of Culture* (University of Chicago Press, 1981). His other books include *Curse of*

Souw: Principles of Daribi Clan Definition and Alliance in New Guinea (University of Chicago Press, 1967), *Habu: The Innovation of Meaning in Daribi Religion* (University of Chicago Press, 1972), *Lethal Speech: Daribi Myth as Symbolic Obviation* (Cornell University Press, 1978), *Symbols That Stand for Themselves* (University of Chicago Press, 1986), and *Asiwinarong: Ethos, Image and Social Power among the Usen Barok of New Ireland* (Princeton University Press, 1986).

INDEX

Aboriginal Australians: commodified, 125; considered homogeneous, 122; dreamtime concept of, 125; film/media production by, 5, 9, 121–138; identity, 121, 122; media affects, 123; self-determination for, 5, 9, 121, 122, 130, 131, 134, 135; state's stance toward, 127, 129–131, 135; television station owned by, 129–131
Adair, John, 126
Advertising, 59–76; anthropology linked to, 71–72; as construct, 61–64; consumption affected by, 59–60, 61; function of, 67; image in, 59–60, 73; manipulation in, 61, 64–65; role of senses in, 73; science fiction compared to, 72; shamanism compared to, 67–68; types of, 62
Allegory, preferred to material, 38n.4
Anderson, Benedict, 124
Anidjar, Gil, 38n.3
Anthropology: advertising linked to, 71–74; as reflexive, 11, 74, 122–123
Appadurai, Arjun, 79, 92, 133
Appiah, Kwame Anthony, 77
Aristotle, 3
Audience: nostalgia implemented by, 83; self-action by, 5
AUSSAT, 129
Australian Broadcasting Corporation, 127
Authority, patriarchial/dynastic, 44, 46, 53, 55
Authorship, multiple, 48, 51, 52, 53, 90
Autonomy, 37

Bali, kinship and personhood in, 106–108
Barth, Lewis M., 24, 25, 26
Barthes, Roland, 1, 2
Bartlett, Donald, 55, 56–57
Battaglia, Debbora, 110, 111–112
Batty, Philip, 128–129, 130–131
Bau ancestors, 81–82, 84
Beckett, Jeremy, 131
Begin, Menachem, 29
Behavior: genes account for, 102–103; relational view of, 99
Benjamin, Walter, 17, 51, 52
Bet-Sahour, 30
Bhabha, Homi, 92, 93
Bible, on circumcision, 24, 25
Bifocalization, 89
Blood libel, 21
Boon, James, 19, 22
Boundaries, 18, 19, 28
Boyarin, Daniel and Jonathan, 6, 7, 8, 11
Braidotti, Rosi, 100
Breckenridge, Carol, 133
Brenkman, John, 87
Burke, Kenneth, 4
Butler, Judith, 6, 37, 38n.3

Campbell, Colin, 113
Carelli, Vincent, 123
Central Australian Aboriginal Media Association (CAAMA), 129
Character, 45; eccentricity replaces, 46–47, 49–50
Christensen, Jerome, 95n.11

Christians, and Jews, 20–22
Circumcision: acceptance of, 28; Biblical
    reference to, 24, 25; as chronological
    boundary, 28; defended, 24–26; as de-
    ferral of father's selfhood, 7; Jewish cri-
    tique of, 30–31; as male menstruation,
    21; as mark of ethnic difference/identity,
    16, 19, 21–23, 31, 32, 34–35; as medi-
    cal procedure, 23; as mutilation, 23, 24;
    among non-Jews, 21, 27; reexperienced,
    36; refused, 22–23; reversal of, 38n.8; as
    sanctification, 24; to symbolically correct
    a flaw, 24–25, 26; as tribal rite, 20
Class: decline of, 45, 46; resentment, 49
Clifford, James, 16, 91
Cohen, Anthony P., 116n.2
Coles, Robert, 53–54
Commoditization, 83, 91, 94n.10, 125
Conformity, threatens tradition, 17
Connolly, William, 27, 31–32, 36–37
Construct/construction, 3, 61–64, 66–67
Consumption, advertising affects, 59–60, 61
Crocodile Dundee, 125
Culture: artifacts of, 80; commodified, 91;
    exported, 91; identity based on, 10, 16,
    123; media affects, 123, 128–129; as pro-
    cess, 95n.13; production of, 123, 128–
    129; publicity affects, 91–92; variability
    in, 110
Cutting, 39n.10

De Man, Paul, 4
Difference, ethnic, 16–41, 79, 121–135; cir-
    cumcision as mark of, 16, 19, 21–23, 31,
    32, 34–35; in global cultural flows, 83,
    91–92, 121, 133–135; head covering as
    mark of, 16–17, 19, 26–27, 29–30, 32–
    33; historical variations in, 27–36; and in-
    digenous media, 121–123, 127–128; and
    the state, 29–30, 79, 87, 90–92, 94,
    124–126, 129–131
DNA testing, 103, 105
Doppelganger, 5, 43, 49. See also Self,
    doubled/parallel
Dreamspeakers Festival, 134
Dreamtime, 20, 125
Dreyfuss, Rochelle, 104, 105–109, 111,
    112, 113, 114, 115
Dumont, Louis, 74
Dundes, Alan, 21
Durkheim, Emile, 73–74
Dutchak, Philip, 128

Dynasty, authority of, 44, 46, 53, 55; and
    eccentricity, 43–58
Eccentricity, 43–58; class resentment labels,
    49; defined, 47–48; and fetishes and ob-
    sessions, 46, 50–57; of Howard Hughes,
    55–57; as identity, 11; lacks self-aware-
    ness/self-consciousness, 48, 50; and patri-
    archal authority, 53; replaces character,
    46–47, 49–50; self is doubled or multi-
    ply authored in, 5, 55–57; as social con-
    struction, 48; and wealth, 48–49, 52–55
Egan, Jeannie Nungarrayi, 132
Enactment, self-performative, 66–67
Entitlement, 53–54
Environment, significance of, 103–104
Ernabella Video Television (EVTV), 127,
    128–129
Essentialism: and anthropology, 11; and fem-
    inist thought, 100, 102; genetic, 9–10,
    105–109, 113–115; of self, 1, 2–4, 7–9,
    103, 117n.11
Ethnicity: as difference (see Difference,
    ethnic); marks self-identity, 16
Ethnography, on self, 3, 12n.6, 12n.7
Europa, Europa, 22

Fabian, Johannes, 72
Family tree, 117n.3
Feld, Steven, 51
Feminist scholarship, 100
Fischer, Michael, 94n.3
Foster, Robert, 8
Foucault, Michel, 4–5

Gardening, urban Trobriand, 79–87; as
    competition, 78–79, 82–84, 85, 88–89;
    as nostalgic, 77, 78, 80, 82; political
    function of, 85–87; as self-problematiza-
    tion, 81
Genetics: behavior accounted for by, 102–
    103; and environment, 103–104; essen-
    tialism of, 9–10, 105–109, 113–114,
    115; fingerprinting by, 103, 105; iden-
    tity/self based on, 9, 103, 104–106,
    108–109; law affected by, 104, 105,
    106, 107; manipulated, 101; mapped,
    102, 105; new, 101–102, 115
Giddens, Anthony, 101
Ginsburg, Faye, 5, 8, 9, 110
Glynn, Freda, 130
Goody, Jack, 98–99

Gould, Stephen Jay, 69
Greenblatt, Stephen, 1
Grobstein, Clifford, 118n.12

Hall, Peter Dobkin, 45
Hamilton, Annette, 122, 124–125
Haraway, Donna, 38, 125
Head covering: boundaries maintained by, 19; to mark male Jewishness, 16–17, 19, 26–27, 29–30, 32–33; political stance indicated by, 29–30
Heelas, Paul, 113
Hegel, G. W. F., 61
Heidegger, Martin, 4
Herrnstein, Richard, 102
Heteroscopy, 68–69
Holland, Agnieszka, 22
Holquist, Michael, 31, 32
Hughes, Howard, 55–57
Hunter, Ian, 81, 87, 94
Hutcheon, Linda, 93, 110

Identity: chosen, 37; cultural, 10, 16, 123; ethnic marks of, 16, 19, 21–23, 31, 32, 34–35; genetics determines, 9, 103, 104–106, 108–109; as given, 36–37; indigenous, 121, 122, 123; Jewish male, 7, 16–42; nostalgia contributes to, 87; without other, 16; publicity as tool of, 87–92, 123; self-, 3, 16, 18 (see also Self); wealth as basis of, 43–44, 46
Image, 67–68, 69–71; in advertising, 59–60, 73; in media, 124–125; is not self, 68; substitutes for effectiveness, 10; Trobriand self-, 6
Imitation/mimesis, 28–29, 52–55
Imparja, 124, 129–131
Inauthenticity, 36–37
Individualism: in kinship, 45–47, 79, 80–83, 86–87, 89, 114–115, 122, 124–125, 127–128; of self, 7–8, 9–10, 93, 106, 107, 108, 133–134
Irony, 112

Jameson, Frederic, 110
Jewish-Christian relationships, 20–22
Jewish male identity, 7, 16–42; circumcision marks, 16, 19, 21–23, 31, 32, 34–35; excluded, 22; as female, 31; head covering marks, 16–17, 26–27, 29–30, 32–33; as other, 32–33; self-made man compared to, 20

Kaluli people, 51–52
Kant, Immanuel, 2
Kinship: in Bali, 107, 108; degree of, 98–99; European/Western vs. non-European/non-Western, 99, 107–108, 112–114; individualism in, 114–115; as past in present, 112–113; and relationships, 113–114; and self, 104; as traditional, 101
Kipa. See Head covering
Kojève, Alexandre, 61
Kronick, Joseph G., 28

Lacan, Jacques, 124
Lacoue-Labarthe, Philippe, 28, 29
Langton, Marcia, 122, 126, 134
Leigh, Michael, 121
Lepani, Charles, 89
Lévi-Strauss, Claude, 67
Lewontin, Richard C., 103–104, 118n.20
Locke, John, 117n.4

McLuhan, Marshall, 64, 126
Magic, 81
Maimonides, 24, 26
Malinowski, Bronislaw K., 79–80
Marcus, George, 5, 8, 11
Margins, as boundaries, 18
Mead, George, 7
Media: Aboriginal, 121, 122–129; connects generations, 123; cultural production affected by, 128–129; identity altered by, 87–92, 123; image in, 124–125; to mediate, 123, 125–126; selfhood negotiated by, 121
Memmi, Albert, 35, 36
Metaphor, preferred to literal, 38n.4
Michaels, Eric, 130; on Aboriginal media, 126–127, 132–133
Mill, John Stuart, 43
Millah. See Circumcision
Minh-Ha, Trinh, 77
Modernism, linked to madness, 48
Modernity, tradition vs., 100–101, 112
Moffat, Tracey, 122
Molnar, Helen, 122
Morris, Paul, 113
Munn, Nancy, 126–127
Murray, D. W., 9

Nancy, Jean-Luc, 28
"National imaginary," 124–125

Nationalism, state, 29
Nazism, 21–22
Need, 64; for a need, 66, 75; want vs., 59–
  60, 63
Nelkin, Dorothy, 104–109, 111, 112, 113,
  114, 115, 118n.19
Nietzsche, Friedrich, 2, 3, 5
Noble, Shlomo, 33
Noel, John, 78–79, 80, 81
Nostalgia, 77–96, 97–120; audience imple-
  ments, 83; function of, 93–94; and identity, 87; irony to avoid, 112; past vs. present in, 110, 111–113; for people or
  places, 111; for reconnection, 78; and relational view of person, 112; and sense of
  loss, 79, 110; substantive, 112–113, 115;
  synthetic, 110, 111–112, 113, 115; tradition vs. modernity in, 79, 100–101, 112;
  of Trobrianders, 77, 78, 80, 82, 110,
  111–112

Objectification, 3, 66
Obsessions, of eccentrics, 46, 50–57
Olender, Maurice, 31
O'Loughlin, Genny, 132
Othello, 21
Other: circumcision of, 21; external, 36;
  internal, 36–38; Jewish male as, 32–33;
  self vs., 7–8, 11, 18

Paine, Robert, 20
Papashvili, George, 73
Papua New Guinea, 78. *See also* Kaluli
  people; Trobrianders
Parfit, Derek, 105
Partisanship, 100
Paul, Saint, on circumcision, 21
Perel, Salomon, 22, 36
Perot, Ross, 39
Peters, Frances, 134
Petronius, 32
Pirandello, Luigi, 51, 55
Pitjantjatjara people, 128–129
Prefiguration, 87
Psychology, on self, 3
Publicity, 87–92; affects culture, 91–92

Rabinow, Paul, 117n.9
Reflexivity, 74
Relation, metaphors for, 103
Relationships, self within, 6–7, 99–100
Ricoeur, Paul, 2, 11
Robertson, Roland, 78, 110

Rose, Nikolas, 97

Sahlins, Marshall, 66
Said, Edward, 124
Salvation, 19–20
Sartre, Jean-Paul, 36
Sass, Louis, 48
Satellite, communications, 123, 129
Schieffelin, Bambi and Edward, 51
Schneider, David, 59
Science fiction, advertising compared to, 72
Scopism, 63–64, 65
Self: definitions of, 106–108; doubled/paral-
  lel, 5, 43, 48, 51, 52, 53; eccentric, 5,
  48, 55–57; and environment, 104; essentialist, 103; ethnic rite as basis of, 7; ethnography on, 3; function of notion of,
  3–4; genetics determines, 9, 103, 104–
  106, 108–109; grounded, 19; incompatible components of, 7; individuated autonomous vs. collective relational, 6, 7–8, 9–
  10, 99–100, 106–108, 111, 112; inner
  vs. outer, 8–9; instability of, 2–3; integration of, 2–3; liberated, 97–98; mainte-
  nance of, 97; media negotiates, 121;
  normalized, 31–32; as not natural, 1; as
  opposed to other, 7–8, 11, 18; production of, 1, 4–5; in psychology, 3; as representation, 2; representation of, 97–98; social action affects, 7; state affects, 29–31;
  technologies of, 4–5; time/chronology
  and, 19–20, 27–29; in tradition, 18;
  transcendent, 3, 9
Self-action, 4–6, 7, 10; by audience, 5;
  spontaneity of, 60, 65
Self-actualization, 97
Self-awareness, 6, 10, 50, 97; hyper, 48
Self-consciousness, 48, 65
Self-determination, 5, 8, 9, 121, 122, 130,
  131, 134, 135
Self-displacement, 79
Self-identity, 3, 16, 18
Self-image, 6
Self-made man, 1, 19–20, 39
Self-problematization, 81
Shamanism, 67–68
Spinoza, Baruch, 30–31
Spiro, Melford, 9
Stacey, Judith, 101
Stanley, Liz, 100, 117n.5
Steele, James, 55, 56–57
Stern, Josef, 24, 25, 26
Strathern, Marilyn, 2, 3, 6, 8, 9, 78

Structuralism, 74–75
Subconscious, 65
Subjectivity, 66; linked to imitation, 28–29
Sutherland, Kathryn, 109

Talmud, 29
Tanami Network, 131–133
Tancredi, Lawrence, 118n.19
Taussig, Michael, 51, 52
Telecasting, 69
Television, 59, 61, 63, 71, 73–74, 124, 126–129
Time, linked to concepts of self, 19–20, 27–29
Toyne, Peter, 132
Tradition: conformity threatens, 17; modernity vs., 100–101, 112; nostalgia salvages, 79
Trawick, Margaret, 12n.6
Trobrianders: on Bau ancestors, 81–82, 84; cultural identity of, 10; gardening competitions of, 78–79, 82–85, 88–89; on magic, 81; nostalgia of, 77, 78, 80, 82, 110, 111–112; on publicity, 87–92; scales of exchange of, 82; self-image of, 6; yams have political functions for, 80, 81, 85–87, 88–91

Tully, James, 117n.4
United Nations Year of Indigenous Peoples, 125
Until the End of the World, 125, 133

VCRs, 123, 126
von Rad, Gerhard, 18

Wagner, Roy, 4, 5–6, 10, 83
Warlpiri Media Association (WMA), 124, 127
Warlpiri people, 126–128, 131–132
Weber, Donald, 90
Weiner, Annette, 86
Weiner, James, 12n.6
Weiss, Brad, 94n.10
Wenders, Wim, 125
Werbner, Richard, 111
White, Luise, 21
Willis, Paul, 58
Wolfson, Elliot R., 24, 25
Worth, Sol, 126

Yarmulke. *See* Head covering
Yams. *See* Gardening
Yothu Yindi, 125
Yuendumu, Australia, 126–127, 131–132

Designer: U.C. Press Staff
Compositor: Maple-Vail Book Manufacturing Group
Text: 10/13 Galliard
Display: Galliard
Printer: Maple-Vail Book Manufacturing Group
Binder: Maple-Vail Book Manufacturing Group